Small Acts of Resistance

Small Acts of Resistance

How Courage, Tenacity, and Ingenuity Can Change the World

Steve Crawshaw and John Jackson

UNION SQUARE PRESS
An imprint of Sterling Publishing Co., Inc.

New York / London
www.sterlingpublishing.com

STERLING and the distinctive Sterling logo are registered trademarks of Sterling Publishing Co., Inc.

Library of Congress Cataloging-in-Publication Data
Crawshaw, Steve.
  Small acts of resistance : how courage, tenacity, and ingenuity can change the world / Steve Crawshaw and John Jackson.
    p. cm.
  Includes bibliographical references and index.
  ISBN 978-1-4027-6807-1 (alk. paper)
  1. Government, Resistance to. 2. Civil disobedience. 3. Human rights. 4. Social action. 5. Social change. I. Jackson, John, 1964- II. Title.
  JC328.3.C73 2010
  322.4--dc22
                                            2010013813

10 9 8 7 6 5 4 3 2 1

Published by Sterling Publishing Co., Inc.
387 Park Avenue South, New York, NY 10016
© 2010 by Steve Crawshaw and John Jackson
Distributed in Canada by Sterling Publishing
^c/o Canadian Manda Group, 165 Dufferin Street
Toronto, Ontario, Canada M6K 3H6
Distributed in the United Kingdom by GMC Distribution Services
Castle Place, 166 High Street, Lewes, East Sussex, England BN7 1XU
Distributed in Australia by Capricorn Link (Australia) Pty. Ltd.
P.O. Box 704, Windsor, NSW 2756, Australia

Sterling ISBN 978-1-4027-6807-1

For information about custom editions, special sales, premium and corporate purchases, please contact Sterling Special Sales Department at 800-805-5489 or specialsales@sterlingpublishing.com.

A person with inner freedom, memory, and fear is that reed, that twig that changes the direction of a rushing river.

—NADEZHDA MANDELSTAM

Contents

Preface by Václav Havel

In 1978, I wrote an essay that explored the untapped "power of the powerless." I described the incalculable benefits that might follow, even in the context of a highly repressive government, if each one of us decided to confront the lies surrounding us, and made a personal decision to live in truth.

Many argued that those ideas were the work of a deluded Czech Don Quixote, tilting at unassailable windmills.

In many ways, that skepticism seemed justified. Leonid Brezhnev, the Soviet leader who just ten years earlier had sent tanks into Czechoslovakia to end political reform, was still in power in the Kremlin. The Solidarity movement—whose remarkable victories in neighboring Poland against unwanted rulers would give comfort to other eastern Europeans and millions of others seeking to live in truth in the years to come—did not yet exist. I myself, like many of my friends, had spent time in jail and would do so again in the years to come.

And yet, just eleven years after I wrote about what ordinary people can achieve by living in truth, I saw and lived through a series of extraordinary victories all across the region, including in my own country. In what came to be known as the velvet revolution, Czechs and Slovaks defied official violence to ensure the speedy collapse of the seemingly impregnable bastion of lies in November 1989. It was all over in barely a week. After the revolution, I was privileged to become the president of my country as it moved into a democratic era.

Today, millions around the world live in circumstances where it might seem that nothing will ever change. But they must remember that the rebellions that took place all across eastern Europe in 1989 were the result of a series of individual actions by ordinary people which together made change inevitable. *Small Acts of Resistance* pays tribute to those who have sought to live in truth, and the impact that can have.

In my lifetime, I have repeatedly seen that small acts of resistance have had incomparably greater impact than anybody could have predicted at the time. Small acts of resistance are not just about the present and the past. I believe they are about the future, too.

Prague
March 2010

Introduction

We have all seen images on our television screens of a political drama unraveling in some distant country. A dictator has fallen, crowds dance in the streets, statues are pulled down, a new flag is hoisted. The camera zooms in, trying to find ways to convey the elation and the exhaustion.

Such moments, however compelling in that instant, often feel like walking into a movie a few minutes before the end. What led to this dramatic moment? How did these people keep going through the long, difficult years? What kept their spirit of defiance alive?

Here we pay tribute to those backstories. Collecting tales from around the world, *Small Acts of Resistance* tells stories—some well-known but many underreported and little recognized in the history books—in which people have found innovative and inspiring ways to challenge violent regimes and confront abuses of power.

We offer accounts of those who refuse to be silenced, showing in the process that it is possible to bring down dictators, change unjust laws, or simply give individuals a renewed sense of their own humanity in the face of those who deny it. Each represents the universal desire to live in dignity and freedom.

The title of this book is in some ways an obvious misnomer. Many of the stories chronicled here are not small acts at all. They involve extraordinary courage, though few of the participants most closely involved saw things that way. At

1

the risk of being beaten, jailed, or even killed in retribution for speaking out, the people in these pages would say they were merely standing up for basic principles. They would claim they were merely doing what anyone else would do. To the rest of us, they stand as powerful reminders that a defiant spirit can make the invincible crack, the unchangeable change.

The people in these stories treat the impossible as the possible that just hasn't happened yet. Some have achieved the change they were struggling for. For others, the biggest change is yet to come.

Steve Crawshaw
John Jackson
New York
March 2010

The Power of Many

Said the boy: "He learnt how quite soft water, by attrition
Over the years will grind strong rocks away.
In other words that hardness must lose the day."
—Bertolt Brecht

Brian: You're all individuals!
Crowd: Yes, we're all individuals! . . .
Man in crowd: I'm not.
—Monty Python's Life of Brian

Strollers Defeat Tanks

The rise of Solidarity, a popular movement created in August 1980 by striking workers in the shipyards of Gdańsk and across Poland, caused panic in the regime that had ruled the country since the Second World War. On December 13, 1981, the Communist authorities put tanks on the streets to stop Solidarity once and for all. Hundreds were arrested; dozens were killed.

Despite the tanks and arrests, Poles organized protests against the ban on Solidarity, including a boycott of the fiction-filled television news. But a boycott of the TV news could not by itself embarrass the government. After all, who could tell how many were obeying the boycott call?

In one small town, they found a way. Every evening, beginning on February 5, 1982, the inhabitants of Świdnik in eastern Poland went on a walkabout. As the half-hour evening news began, the streets would fill with Świdnikians, who chatted, walked, and loafed. Before going out, some placed their switched-off television set in the window, facing uselessly onto the street. Others went a step further. They placed their disconnected set in a stroller or a builder's wheelbarrow, and took the television itself for a nightly outing.

"If resistance is done by underground activists, it's not you or me," one Solidarity supporter later noted. "But if you see your neighbors taking their TV for a walk, it makes you feel part of something. An aim of dictatorship is to make you feel isolated. Świdnik broke the isolation and built confidence."

The TV-goes-for-a-walk tactics, which spread to other towns and cities, infuriated the government. But the authorities felt powerless to retaliate. Going for a walk was not, after all, an official crime under the criminal code.

Eventually, the curfew was brought forward from 10 p.m. to 7 p.m., thus forcing Świdnikians to stay at home during the 7:30 news, or risk being arrested or shot.

The citizens of Świdnik responded by going for a walk during the earlier edition of the news at 5 p.m. instead.

Just as it was difficult (unless everybody went for a walk) to be sure that Poles were *not* watching the television news, it was hard to know how many people *were* listening to programs that criticized the government. Solidarity found a way around that problem, too.

Radio Solidarity broadcast illegal news bulletins that countered official propaganda. But nobody could be sure how many people were listening to those underground reports. Opinion polls were, under the circumstances, unthinkable. So the Solidarity broadcasters devised an experiment. They asked people to switch the lights on and off in their apartment at a certain point in the program.

There was an obvious risk. If you were the only one on your block with your lights blinking, that would advertise to police officers in the vicinity: "Look, a lawbreaker lives here!"

Dissident Konstanty Gebert was walking down a street in the Polish capital, Warsaw, during the broadcast. As he walked, he noticed the lights in a ground-floor apartment starting to flash on and off. As he stepped back, he realized that the whole building was flashing. He turned to look behind him and saw block after block lit up like Christmas trees, all the way down the street. Reports that night said that buildings flashed on and off throughout the city. Gebert said: "You can't imagine the feeling of elation."

As for the authorities: Short of arresting all the inhabitants of Warsaw, there was little they could do.

*
* *

Even on the most solemn occasions, Solidarity supporters found ways of undermining Poland's detested rulers. In 1984, Soviet leader Yuri Andropov died. Scheduled programming was interrupted for live coverage of the funeral, including a speech by Andropov's aged successor, Konstantin Chernenko, speaking from the top of Lenin's mausoleum on Red Square in Moscow.

The official broadcast was soon interrupted, as seen in Grzegorz Linkowski's 2006 documentary *Stroll with the Television News*. Instead of Chernenko's loyal mumblings ("Yuri Andropov, a glorious son of the Communist Party, has departed this life . . ."), Polish viewers suddenly heard a different announcer break in: "Here is the TV version of Radio Solidarity. Good evening, ladies and gentlemen . . ." whereupon a list of arrested activists and a series of opposition demands followed.

Polish viewers were delighted. The authorities were not. The secret police couldn't identify the culprits. The embarrassment for the government—and the delight of everybody else—remained.

The TV-filled strollers, the flashing lights, and the interrupted funeral kept the flame of Polish hope alive—with dramatic implications in the years to come. The immovable regime crumbled within just a few years.

The Great One-Liner

The military junta that ruled Uruguay from 1973 was intolerant in the extreme. Hundreds of thousands fled into exile. Political opponents were jailed. Torture was the order of the day. On occasion, even concerts of classical music were seen as subversive threats. A performance of Ravel's *Piano Concerto for Left Hand* was canceled because the title sounded leftishly dangerous. Meanwhile, however, a remarkable small protest took place at soccer games throughout the twelve long years of military rule.

Whenever the band struck up the national anthem before major games, thousands of Uruguayans in the stadium joined in unenthusiastically. This stubborn failure to sing loudly was rebellion enough. But, from the generals' point of view, there was worse to come. At one point, the anthem declares, *Tiranos temblad!*—"May tyrants tremble!" Those words served as the cue for the crowds in the stadium suddenly to bellow in unison: *"Tiranos temblad!"* as they waved their flags. After that brief, excited roar, they continued to mumble their way through to the end of the long anthem.

The authorities could not arrest everyone in the stadium. Nor could they cancel games or drop the singing of the national anthem. The junta toyed with the idea of removing the *tiranos temblad!* line from public performances of the anthem, but that proved too embarrassing. Why, after all, would the generals remove words from a beloved nineteenth-century hymn, unless they believed that *they* might be the tyrants in question?

The military rulers were thus obliged to suffer the embarrassment until 1985, when they and their friends lost power. Democracy won.

Today, the national anthem can be sung at Uruguayan soccer games in full and without fear. Leaders of the junta have been jailed for the crimes committed during their years in power. The former tyrants tremble.

Turnips and Revolution

Boycott is a widely understood form of social, economic, and political action. Everybody now takes the word for granted. But it was not plucked out of thin air. Once upon a time there was Captain Charles Cunningham Boycott. Captain Boycott was a much-disliked land agent for Lord Erne, an absentee landlord in County Mayo in the west of British-ruled Ireland.

On September 23, 1880, "as if by one sudden impulse" (in the words of the *Connaught Telegraph*), Boycott's servants walked out on him, in protest against unjust rents and evictions. Boycott and his family found themselves obliged to milk their own cows, shoe their own horses, and till their own fields. Shopkeepers refused to serve Boycott and his family. The post office stopped delivering mail to him. Boycott was isolated and powerless to retaliate, to the dismay of his supporters. In London, an editorial in the *Times* complained: "A more frightful picture of triumphant anarchy has never been presented in any community pretending to be civilized and subjected to law."

One of the organizers of the action, James Redpath, realized that no single word existed to describe this successful form of ostracism. To bolster the political impact of these actions, he decided that needed to change. As Redpath recounts in his 1881 memoir *Talks About Ireland*, he asked the sympathetic priest, Father John O'Malley, for advice: "[O'Malley] looked down, tapped his big forehead, and said: 'How would it be to call it to Boycott him?'"

In *Captain Boycott and the Irish*, Joyce Marlow describes how a pro-English volunteer force came to help the beleaguered Boycott, guarded by a detachment of a thousand soldiers. Their supplies included fourteen gallons of whiskey, thirty pounds of tobacco, and four foghorns. After a few weeks of digging vegetables in the rain, however, they abandoned Boycott once more. Boycott fled to England. He never returned. In due course, Ireland gained its independence.

Meanwhile, the name of an obscure land agent in the west of Ireland has gone global in the dictionaries. General Augusto Pinochet's regime suffered from those who were ready to *boicotear* Chilean apples and wine in protest against repression by the military junta in Chile in the 1970s. Poles protesting against the Communist imposition of martial law in 1981 declared a *bojkot* of the television news (including with televisions in wheelbarrows, as described above). Russians talk of *boikotirovat*, and the French declare *un boycott*. And all because of some local difficulties involving the Irish turnip harvest of 1880.

And Then They All Fall Down

There is a familiar pattern of censorship in authoritarian countries. An author publishes a piece of work that the government dislikes. Publishers and authors are threatened, fined, or jailed. The publisher goes out of business, other brave authors or publishers are deterred, and the regime lives happily ever after (for a time, at least).

And then there's the Turkish way: togetherness as a defiant criminal act.

The principle is simple. It is grounded in the knowledge that while prosecuting one or two people is easy, prosecuting a hundred or a thousand people for the same crime eventually becomes more of a pain for the government than for the would-be defendants.

In 1995, the distinguished writer Yaşar Kemal was charged under antiterrorism laws in connection with an article he published in the German magazine *Der Spiegel* about brutality against Kurds in southeast Turkey. So far, so bad for Kemal. Fellow writers provided Kemal with much-needed solidarity, however. As Kemal himself publicly declared at the time, "Time will tell that it is my prosecutors who are on trial."

He was proved right. Authors published a joint book with ten banned articles—including Kemal's. More than a thousand people were named as collective publishers. The prosecutor opened a trial against 185 prominent intellectuals. But it all became too cumbersome and politically embarrassing. After two years of the authorities looking foolish, the trial was dropped.

The would-be defendants were dissatisfied, however, with the authorities' failure to prosecute. Şanar Yurdatapan, the composer and author who coordinated the campaign, compared the tactics with a children's tug-of-war. "Some children hold one end of a thick rope and others hold the other end. They start pulling at the same time to see which group is stronger. But what happens if one group simply lets go of the rope?" he asked. "The others fall down altogether and everybody laughs at them."

The accused demanded that the prosecutor take action. In Yurdatapan's words, "The rabbit was following the hound."

From 2001 onwards, a volume titled *Freedom of Thought* was published annually—bringing together those with very different views, left and right, secular and Islamist. The lawbreakers cut a birthday cake, sent pieces to the judges and the prosecutors, and handed a copy of the offending volume to the prosecutor.

From the government's point of view, this rabbit-chases-hound business—turning upside down the familiar world, where defendants want to walk free and prosecutors try to ensure that they don't—was most annoying, especially when it continued to spread. Tens of thousands of people have become "copublishers" of banned writings in recent years.

Dirty Linen in Public

It might not seem that an act of public laundry could unsettle a president with a well-deserved reputation for inflexibility, corruption, and brutality. But mass washing ceremonies were a key element in getting rid of Peru's unpopular president, Alberto Fujimori, after more than a decade in power.

In May 2000, thousands started gathering every Friday, from noon until three, on Plaza Mayor in the Peruvian capital, Lima. The main focus: washing the red-white-red-striped flag. The crowds wanted to show that Peru, and its flag, had become badly soiled.

The authorities reacted with intimidation and threats. Vladimiro Lenin Montesinos, head of the security services, complained about this "cancer," and suggested that the flag washers were terrorists. But still the *lava la bandera*—wash-the-flag—protests continued. As actor and protester Miguel Iza declared: "I just want a clean country."

The protests spread across the country. Hundreds of thousands took part. Eventually, the *lava la bandera* action achieved its aim. Five months after the protests began, Fujimori stepped down. (He resigned by fax while on a visit to Japan.) Washing the flag, said the Peruvian daily *La República* in its end-of-millennium roundup, was "a ritual that we Peruvians will never forget."

In 2009, Fujimori (extradited from Chile two years earlier) was jailed for twenty-five years for the killings committed under his rule. Peruvian flags are now clean.

2

Mischief with a Purpose

The human race has unquestionably one really
effective weapon—laughter . . . Against the assault of
laughter nothing can stand.

—Mark Twain

Laughter and tears are both responses to frustration
and exhaustion. I myself prefer to laugh, since there
is less cleaning up to do afterward.

—Kurt Vonnegut

High-Fidelity Fast Food

One of the extraordinary things about human events is that the unthinkable becomes thinkable.

—Salman Rushdie

Police in a one-party state have a more or less simple task. If people criticize the government, they are either harassed or arrested. The system is clear-cut and well understood by arresters and arrested alike.

Things get more complicated when citizens become implausibly loyal.

In Poland in the 1980s, after the banning of the independent Solidarity movement (as described in Chapter 1), there were countless demonstrations against the Communist regime. Then there was the Orange Alternative—which demonstrated *in support* of Communism, carrying banners demanding an eight-hour workday for the secret police and showering police cars with flowers.

Everybody knew that such spontaneous support was unthinkable, and understood the pro-Communist sentiment as an unkind joke. It was, however, embarrassing for the government to admit that aloud.

A "pro-Communist" demonstration on the occasion of the seventieth anniversary of the Russian Revolution in 1987 began with the rousing call, "It is time to break the passivity of the popular masses!" All demonstrators were asked to wear something Communist red: red shoes, red scarf, or at least red lipstick. Those who had nothing red to wear queued up for ketchup-smeared pizza sticks from a nearby fast-food stall, later holding the color-coded food aloft. The police closed the stall down and a customer who asked for ketchup only, never mind the pizza stick, was arrested.

The Orange Alternative also mocked the regime by addressing people's basic needs. At a 1988 event called "Who's Afraid of Toilet Paper?" single sheets of toilet paper (which, like so much else, was unavailable in Polish shops at that time) were distributed free to passersby, thus mocking the official shortages. Another event involved the free distribution of sanitary napkins (also unavailable in stores) on International Women's Day. Again, arrests were made.

That same year, the government finally agreed to talks with Solidarity. Those talks led to contested elections, which had previously seemed unthinkable. Solidarity's victory in the elections of June 1989 was so overwhelming that the Communists were forced to hand over power. In August, Poland gained the first popularly elected prime minister in the Soviet bloc.

Three months later, not least as a consequence of the defeat of Communism in Poland, the Berlin Wall fell. Illegal ketchup and free toilet paper had each played a part.

Which Side Are You On?

In Oxford and other British university cities, an unusual set of graffiti appeared above pairs of Barclays Bank cash dispensers in 1984. Above one ATM was spray-painted the word BLACKS. Above the other: WHITES ONLY.

The graffiti changed nothing, of course, in terms of who could use which cash machine. Customers were free to choose whichever ATM they preferred. Black customers could line up at the WHITES ONLY machine if they wished to. Whites could take cash from the BLACKS machine.

The black-and-white labeling left people faintly unsettled, however. And unsettled was all that was needed. The graffiti made many of those lining up at the black-vs.-white machines feel uncomfortable about Barclays' well-publicized involvement in the South African system of apartheid, where signs proclaiming NET BLANKES—Whites Only—were at that time the order of the day.

Fewer graduates applied to work at Barclays, so as not to be tainted by the black-white division that the bank seemed to represent. Barclays' once lucrative share of UK student accounts plummeted from 27 percent to 15 percent of the market. In 1986, the banking giant admitted defeat at the hands of the graffiti sprayers and their allies. The Barclays pullout became one of the most high-profile and punishing acts of divestment suffered by the South African regime.

Nelson Mandela, imprisoned for life because of his rejection of the government's racist policies, was released after twenty-seven years in 1990. Democratic elections were held in 1994. The Barclays graffiti were scrubbed away. Barclays returned to South Africa in 2005.

All Dressed Up and Nowhere to Go

In Iran, being a mullah isn't easy. The men of God may have ruled the country for decades, following the revolution that overthrew the Shah in 1979, but they can't seem to catch a cab.

Taxi drivers in Tehran regularly refuse to stop if they see turbaned men of God standing by the side of the road.

Any other passenger, yes—but not a mullah. The mullahs can stand and wave for as long as they like. Somehow, the taxis are always just too busy to stop.

To the delight of Iranian audiences, that small act of cab-driving defiance was immortalized in Kamal Tabrizi's popular 2004 film *Lizard*, which tells the story of the petty criminal Reza the Lizard (so called because he can climb vertical walls), who escapes from jail disguised in a mullah's (stolen) clothes. Taxis refuse to stop for Reza, the mullah look-alike, in a scene familiar to Iranians from daily life.

Iranians lined up around the block to see *Lizard*, roaring with laughter at the disrespectful film, whose story line suggested that this petty criminal behaved with more moral decency than the supposedly pious mullahs. *Lizard* became the biggest box office hit in Iranian history.

The authorities banned the smash hit after just a few weeks, but by then it was too late. Those who hadn't already seen it during its brief run in the movie theaters watched it at home on pirated DVDs.

And the real-life taxis still don't stop when the mullahs want them to.

Women are banned from attending soccer games in Iran—a rule allegedly intended to shield them from bad language and possible violence on the part of the male sporting fans. In defiance of the ban, women still sometimes try to gain admission to the games, despite the risk of arrest. Public questioning of the ban is prohibited. But Jafar

Panahi, an award-winning filmmaker who has more than once been arrested for daring to speak out, was determined to find a way to address the issue.

Panahi envisioned making a comedy about six defiant young female fans arrested for trying to get into a big game between Iran and Bahrain in 2005. He knew, however, the film proposal would never make it past the censors. So he offered authorities a bland, acceptable script, which gained him the official approval he needed. And then he went ahead and made a different film, the one he had always planned to make.

In *Offside*, a group of women are arrested after attempting to sneak into a soccer game. They are imprisoned in an improvised cattle pen tantalizingly close to the game, and are able to hear the sounds of the crowd. But they are forbidden to move just a few yards to watch the game. The guards explain that the women cannot enter the stadium because of the obscene language they might hear. "We promise we won't listen," the women reply.

One woman urgently needs to relieve herself. But there are only men's toilets in the stadium. (Women, after all, are not supposed to be there in the first place.) As the woman skips with increasingly frantic desperation from one foot to the other, one of the guards finally offers a solution: to disguise herself as a man.

The woman does so, covering her face with a poster of an Iranian soccer star. Thus masked, she is allowed to walk to the toilet. The men are all thrown out, so that the disguised woman has the guarded bathroom all to herself. She promptly escapes.

With its sly disrespect for the official rules, *Offside* was predicted to break box office records. Panahi can hardly have been surprised when the film—so different from the script that the censors had approved—was banned from public release in 2006.

Like *Lizard*, the subversive *Offside* quickly gained popularity when distributed on unauthorized DVDs. The characters inspired real-life imitations, too. Women stood outside the national soccer stadium and chanted, "We don't want to be *Offside!*"

Of Dogs and Dictators

In September 2007, tens of thousands took to the streets to protest against the lawlessness of the military regime in Burma (officially known as Myanmar). (See the photo on pages 24 and 25.) The protests were triggered by a sudden sharp increase in the cost of fuel, but quickly broadened to calls for basic rights and freedoms. The military beat, arrested, and killed protesters. According to the UN, at least thirty-one people died. It became too dangerous to venture onto the streets, which were patrolled by the military. But the imaginative Burmese found a way around that problem: In Rangoon and other cities, they promoted the legions of stray urban dogs to the ranks of protesters.

Dogs are regarded as lowly creatures in Burmese culture. Being reborn as a dog suggests that you were up to no good in a previous life. To hurl a hefty insult in Burmese, throw the word *dog* or *dog's mother* in somewhere, and you won't go wrong.

Perhaps in an attempt to improve their chances in the next life, stray dogs began to be seen roaming around Rangoon with pictures of the military leader, Than Shwe, and images of other senior leaders tied around their necks.

Throughout the city and to the delight of its residents, troops were seen chasing the protesting mutts down, in a vain attempt to rescue the generals' irretrievably low esteem.

The Irrawaddy, published in neighboring Thailand, quoted a resident as saying with approval: "They seem quite good at avoiding arrest."

"Dress conservatively" was the instruction from Burma's military junta to those celebrating the country's traditional annual water festival. This was the result.

Credit: Khin Maung Win/AP

3

A Sporting Chance

Some people believe football is a matter of life and death. I can assure you it is much more important than that.
—Bill Shankly, manager of the Liverpool soccer team

Team Dream

West Africa's Ivory Coast has long been known as the world's largest producer of cocoa. In recent years, however, it has been better known for its dangerous instability and for a brutal conflict. Following a 2002 coup, the country was divided between the South, which remained loyal to the government, and the rebel-held North. Political and ethnic divisions ran deep. As is so often the case in such conflicts, civilians suffered most—enduring mutilation, rape, and murder in the violent clashes of the civil war. Even as the war wound down, suspicion between the two sides seemed impossible to overcome.

One man helped change that.

For several years, the conflict made it impossible to travel from one end of the country to the other. Didier Drogba, Ivorian-born international soccer star, was determined that his splintered nation should be reunited. And he wanted soccer to play a role.

In addition to playing for the Chelsea team in London, Drogba was captain of the Ivorian national team, the Elephants. He insisted that the team should be ethnically mixed, and achieved that goal. When the integrated Ivory Coast team qualified for the 2006 World Cup, Ivorians from all over the country united in cheering the win.

Then, in 2007, Drogba went a step further with a simple, revolutionary move: He declared that the qualifying game for the African Nations Cup would be held in Bouaké, the rebel capital in the North, which had remained off-limits for government forces, even after a March 2007 peace treaty. Drogba was categorical: "3 June will be a memorable day. It will be the victory for Ivory Coast football, the victory of the Ivory Coast people and quite simply there will be peace."

People who had been unable to reconcile their differences for five years came together in Bouaké—for a soccer game. Twenty-five thousand Ivorians watched together as Ivory Coast defeated Madagascar 5–0. The game was capped off by a goal in the final minute by Drogba himself. An explosion of celebrations followed.

The national victory wasn't just about the goals scored. Austin Merrill, present in the stadium that day, later wrote: "You didn't have to look hard to see that there was much more at stake than just a soccer match. On this day, the Beautiful Game had reunited a country."

Christophe Diecket, an official with the National Football Federation, described his reaction to the game: "I got goose bumps. My wife cried. The people on TV cried," he said. "We Ivorians, we had this abscess, a sickness, but we had no way to lance it to get better. It couldn't have been done by anyone else. Only Drogba." As one front-page Ivorian headline declared after the game: "Five goals to erase five years of war."

Humbling an Empire

In the 2001 Bollywood film *Lagaan* ("Land Tax"), an Indian village takes on the might of the nineteenth-century British Empire through a game of cricket. The wager of the game? The villagers will pay extra taxes if they lose, and none if they win. The Oscar-nominated film is full of suspense, as the future of the village hangs in the balance, but the story is fiction. (In the end, of course, the village wins.)

Ninety years earlier, a different—and this time very real—sporting story gripped India. In 1911, the Mohun Bagan ("Sweet Group") soccer team won victory after victory against English teams. Increasingly, the victories fired the passions of India's independence movement against the British Raj. When Mohun Bagan reached the final against the East Yorkshire Regiment (which had, until then, dominated the Indian Football League), tens of thousands traveled from all over the country to see the historic game on July 29, 1911.

There were no proper stands. Spectators at the back of the crowd could barely see what was happening on the field. Those with privileged positions at the front communicated the score to those farther back by flying kites. In a riveting game, the Mohun Bagan players competed barefoot against the booted British team.

The Indian team came from a goal down to score twice in the last five minutes. The historic 2–1 victory by the colonized over the colonizers triggered massive celebrations, on and off the field. When the final whistle sounded, shirts, hats, handkerchiefs, sticks, and umbrellas flew through the air. There were whoops, screams, and dances.

This was not just a sporting victory. The *Nayak,* a Calcutta newspaper, exulted: "It fills every Indian with joy and pride to know that rice-eating, malaria-ridden, barefooted Bengalis have got the better of beef-eating, Herculean, booted John Bull in the peculiarly English sport."

The British decision later the same year to move the imperial capital from Calcutta to Delhi was partly to preempt further humiliation in Bengal, where soccer and proindependence sentiment had become so intertwined.

The poet Achintya Kumar Sengupta wrote, "Mohun Bagan is not a football team. It is an oppressed country, rolling in the dust, which has just started to raise its head."

A soccer game had unsettled an empire.

A Fighter's Peace

"Ain't no Viet Cong ever called me nigger."

That single sentence, uttered by boxer Muhammad Ali in 1966, is packed with all the qualities of the man as a fighter: the speed at which it is understood, its razor-sharp accuracy, the courage of saying it, the power of its impact.

Even as America was embroiled in a war in distant Vietnam, protesters at home were waging a nonviolent struggle in which the civil rights movement tried to dismantle the racist institutions that comprised America's own version of apartheid. Ali's single sentence exposed the contradiction of fighting in the name of freedom on the other side of the world when people were being brutalized and beaten for trying to win basic rights on the streets at home.

The twenty-five-year-old world heavyweight champion was provocative. He was eloquent and forceful, and he knew that the world listened to what he had to say. And so, as one of the most famous men on the planet and at the height of his boxing prowess, he made a remarkable sacrifice.

In the spring of 1967, Ali was drafted into the U.S. armed forces. He likely could have avoided direct combat by fighting in exhibition matches to serve out his term in the military. For Ali, however, the principle mattered. With reference to his hometown of Louisville, Kentucky, Ali asked: "Why should they ask me to put on a uniform and go ten thousand miles from home and drop bombs and bullets on brown people in Vietnam, while so-called Negro people in Louisville are treated like dogs and denied simple human rights? No, I am not going ten thousand miles from home to help murder and burn another poor nation, simply to continue the domination of white slave masters of the darker people of the world."

On April 28, 1967, Ali refused to take the traditional step forward at the military induction center when his name was called. He knew he was risking jail and his career, but he also knew he was setting an example. Supporters outside the induction center chanted: "If he won't go, we won't go!" Other black athletes followed his lead.

Ali was arrested, stripped of his championship title, and banned from boxing. He was convicted of refusing induction into the armed forces and received the maximum sentence—five years in prison (overturned on appeal) and a $10,000 fine. His enforced exile from boxing lasted three years—a time that might well have given him the best years of his boxing career.

The image of the Ali we know now has been partly sanitized with the passage of time. But the power of his personality and provocative statements and the controversial decisions he made as a young man challenged American society. Actor Richard Harris made a simple contrast: "Every single boxer in the world would sell their soul to become the heavyweight champion of the world. What did Ali do? He regained his soul by giving the title up."

Kicking Back

*I have cherished the ideal of a democratic and free society in
which all people live together in harmony and with equal
opportunities. It is an ideal which I hope to live for, and to see
realized. But, my lord, if it needs be, it is an ideal for which
I am prepared to die.*

—NELSON MANDELA AT HIS TRIAL IN 1964, BEFORE RECEIVING
A LIFE SENTENCE AND BEING SENT TO ROBBEN ISLAND

Johannesburg, South Africa. Dawn on election day, April 27, 1994.
Credit: Tom Stoddart/Getty Images

Robben Island, a windswept piece of rock a few miles off Cape Town, has become an internationally notorious symbol of the white South African system of apartheid. Nelson Mandela—apartheid's best-known opponent, who described the system as "moral genocide"—spent twenty-seven years behind bars, mostly on Robben Island, for his part in confronting the regime. He was joined at the prison by many of his comrades in the struggle. The prisoners, black and white, shared a common belief that the racist system was wrong. They were also united in their determination that their spirits would not be broken by their incarceration.

One obvious form of resistance was through the power of education. "Robben Island was known as 'the University' because of what we learned from each other," Mandela later wrote in his autobiography, *Long Walk to Freedom*. But the prisoners found an additional weapon for defying attempts to break them: organized games of soccer.

The authorities were initially contemptuous when inmates demanded the right to play soccer in 1964—the same year that a forty-six-year-old Mandela arrived on the island. As described in Chuck Korr and Marvin Close's *More Than Just a Game*, the warden repeatedly punished those who asked to play soccer by canceling their food rations. Still, the prisoners refused to back down from their demand.

This tiny struggle to be allowed to play a game became a microcosm of much larger battles for dignity and human rights on the South African mainland. The unifying influence of the struggle to be allowed to play soccer, which brought together competing political factions, served as a reminder that the potential benefits of the game went well beyond the playing field.

Even as the authorities continued to refuse, the prisoners continued to insist. Week after week, they discussed how they would organize the game, if permission were ever granted. In 1966, a window of opportunity finally opened in the form of a visit by the International Committee of the Red Cross. Prisoners complained to the foreign visitors. After three years of rebuffs and reprisals, the authorities made the apparently minimal concession in December 1967. From now on, prisoners would be allowed to play a single weekly game.

Because of the prisoners' poor rations and hard labor in the island's stone quarries, many barely had the strength to play. They played barefoot. But what they lacked in resources they made up for in energy and organizational skills.

Eight clubs were formed, under the umbrella name of the Makana Football Association—named after a warrior the British had banished to Robben Island 150 years earlier, in 1819. The Makana Football Association elected its officials. Members of the association drafted a constitution. A Protest and Misconduct Committee was created, granting full rights of appeal with all due process. Organizing soccer became a kind of dry run for the apparently unthinkable option—the eventual formation of a government in a democratic South Africa. The contrast to the lawless apartheid system, which had put the men behind bars, was conscious and striking.

Preserving a sense of identity was important, too. Wardens on Robben Island addressed prisoners by numbers or with abusive epithets. The Robben Island soccer records, by contrast, used the formal *Mr.* Communications on soccer-related matters included a full postal address, with cell and cell-block number. The letters always ended "Yours in sports."

As Robben Island prisoner Anthony Suze noted later: "It is amazing to think that a game that people take for granted all around the world was the very same game that gave a group of prisoners sanity—and in a way gave us the resolve to carry on the struggle."

Nelson Mandela, the world's most famous political prisoner, was finally released in February 1990. Four years later, on April 27, 1994, millions of voters queued patiently to vote, as South Africa held historic elections in which the black majority was allowed to vote for the first time. The formerly banned African National Congress won an overwhelming victory, and Mandela became the country's president. April 27 became a national holiday, known as Freedom Day.

And yet, even after the 1994 elections, South Africa remained unstable. White extremists—including those within the still unreformed security forces—refused to accept that the apartheid era was over. They were prepared to use violence to reverse history. Mandela was convinced that sport could defuse the brewing violence. Sport (including a series of sporting boycotts) had helped end apartheid. Now Mandela wanted sport to help bring peace, too.

Most South African blacks saw rugby, overwhelmingly played and watched by whites, as the sport of the oppressor— "apartheid in a tracksuit." Mandela was determined to change that perception.

He had a twofold strategy. In advance of the 1995 Rugby World Cup, which South Africa was hosting for the first time, Mandela wooed the South African rugby team, the Springboks—and their white supporters—in one of the most remarkable charm offensives the world has ever seen. "Sport has the power to change the world," he said. "It is more powerful than governments in breaking down racial barriers."

Mandela wanted the white resisters of change to lose their fear of black-majority rule. And, at the same time, he sought to persuade blacks to see the team as an integral part of the new South Africa, deserving of black support. Most of Mandela's own supporters were initially unconvinced, and were dismayed by the president's overtures to the former oppressors. Mandela talked later of the hostile response from his own supporters when he dared to put on a Springbok cap early in the World Cup tournament: "They booed me! They booed me down!"

Justice Bekebeke, a former inmate of apartheid jails, was one of many who could not bring themselves to support the long-loathed team. He later told John Carlin, author of *Playing the Enemy: Nelson Mandela and the Game That Made a Nation*, "I was an admirer of Mandela. But the Springboks, that Springbok emblem those people took such pride in: I hated it. It remained for me a potent and loathsome symbol of apartheid." (Carlin's book became the basis for Clint Eastwood's 2009 film *Invictus*.)

Still, Mandela refused to give up. And, with each new South African victory in the championships, popular support for the once-hated team continued to grow. On June 24, 1995 came the final—South Africa's Springboks against New Zealand's All Blacks. Mandela walked out on to the field wearing the Springboks' green jersey and cap.

The mostly white crowd—many of whom had until now refused to acknowledge Mandela as their democratically elected leader—cheered his name as never before. The white rugby team sang the South African liberation anthem, *Nkosi sikelele Afrika*—"God Bless Africa"—whose Xhosa-language phrases they had been practicing to get their tongues around for weeks.

On both sides, millions were won over—in the stadium, in the townships, and around the country. Even Justice

Bekebeke was swayed by Mandela's strategy. "In my township, among my people, there was not a single rugby lover. Yet on that day, we were celebrating as South Africans, as one nation," Bekebeke said. "And we knew, deep down, that the Springboks had won because we had willed them to win. It was a phenomenal day."

4
Cheating the Censor

You can cage the singer, but not the song.
—Harry Belafonte

In Burma, even to be seen holding Aung San Suu Kyi's image is an act of resistance.

Hidden Messages

Among the basic freedoms to which men aspire that their lives might be full and uncramped, freedom from fear stands out as both a means and an end.

—Aung San Suu Kyi

The brutality of the Burmese military junta made international headlines following the massacre of hundreds of peaceful prodemocracy protesters in 1988. When, in 1990, the party of opposition politician Aung San Suu Kyi won an overwhelming election victory, the generals ignored the results—jailing, torturing, and even killing those who dared to speak out.

Aung San Suu Kyi was kept under house arrest. Pinning her picture up, in public or in private, became grounds for arrest. All the more startling, then, was the design of a modest banknote that the government commissioned and published at that time.

Unfortunately for the regime, the designer of the new one-kyat note was a political supporter of Aung San Suu Kyi's. He saw an opportunity for subversion in his task. He knew the note must include an image of Aung San Suu Kyi's late father—General Aung San. The general was the founder of the Burmese army, and was revered by the Burmese for his pivotal role in securing his country's independence from British colonial rule.

The designer engraved the image of the general in the watermark. As he drew, however, he subtly softened the sharp line of the soldier's jawline. He also used a light hand when drawing the general's eyes, nose, and mouth. From these slight, almost imperceptible changes emerged a powerful form of sedition: The face of the father was gently transformed into the face of the daughter.

The censors approved the design—failing to notice that the watermark resembled the daughter more than the father. With the subversive image in place, the banknote was printed, distributed, and put into mass circulation.

In tea shops and pagodas across the country in the weeks and months to come, people whispered to each other as they studied the new note with its hidden portrait of "The Lady," as Aung San Suu Kyi is known to her compatriots.

The act of subversion wasn't limited to the main portrait. The floral design consists of four circles of eight petals—eight around eight around eight around eight, echoing the date of Burma's democratic "four-eights" uprising that began on 8/8/88. Some observers believe there are as many as eleven hidden messages in the design of the banknote.

Everyone agreed on one thing: The most powerful image was the watermark, showing the face of Aung San Suu Kyi—whose name translates as Bright Collection of Small Victories. People held the banknote up with disbelief and pride.

The generals did not feel pride. The subtly defiant one-kyat note was withdrawn from circulation and possession of the banknote became illegal. Those who kept their note still treasure it. It is known as the "democracy note."

The unwillingness of the Burmese people to submit to the brutality of the ruling generals has not diminished over the years. That became clear with the so-called "saffron revolution" of 2007, a series of mass demonstrations led by monks. As described in Chapter 2, at least thirty-one protesters were killed, and thousands more were beaten and jailed. Honest discussion of the protests in the official media was unthinkable. But brave Burmese found ways of getting messages through, even in the most repressive of times.

The caption to a photograph published in the progovernment *New Light of Myanmar* newspaper on October 10, 2007 claimed that the picture showed a demonstration in London against the war in Iraq. The Burmese censors liked the sound of that. But they neglected to check the photograph itself—which showed nothing of the kind. Instead, it showed a peaceful protest in support of the monks and the huge protests for Burmese democracy which had been so harshly repressed in previous weeks. The logo of the Burma Campaign UK, which the government loves to loathe, was clearly visible in the photograph. There was no mention of Iraq.

The courageous placement of the subversive photograph gave Burmese readers a signal of international solidarity, which only infuriated the ruling generals—and gave comfort to ordinary Burmese.

Quantum of Solace

A popular science article, published in the Iranian daily *Jam e Jam* on April 12, 2007, explained Albert Einstein's theory of relativity. The article seemed innocuous enough. But the accompanying photograph of Einstein at the blackboard also included a digital tweak: a message to President Mahmoud Ahmadinejad himself, who famously defied international calls to halt his nuclear program for many years. The Persian message scrawled on Einstein's blackboard read, "What a mistake I made when I started this whole atomic business. Dear Mahmoud, I beg you to give it up!"

The president and his officials—who have jailed journalists for less—were unamused that such a message had slipped through unnoticed until it was too late. But the Photoshop rebel covered his or her tracks well. The authorities never identified who was responsible for such public impertinence against the Iranian leader.

Laughable News

In Nepal in 2005, all freedoms were seemingly crushed overnight. King Gyanendra (who became king by default after his nephew went on a drunken shootout, killing the king, queen, and a clutch of other royals) dismissed the parliament and declared a state of emergency. Elected politicians were arrested and telephone lines were cut to prevent communication with the outside world. Nepal became one of the most strictly censored countries in the world. The country's journalists remained uncowed, however, despite threats and arrests.

The journalists of Radio Sagarmatha, for example, fought to get the news out by calling it something else—essentially, "not news." The standard Nepali word for news is *samachar*. But there is also a less formal word, *haalchal,* meaning a casual conversation. So Mohan Bista, station director of Radio Sagarmatha, had an idea. As he told an interviewer later, "We started calling our news broadcasts *haalchal* instead."

The authorities soon caught on to the "It's not news, just chitchat!" ploy, threatening to close down Radio Sagarmatha unless it ended its news-as-*haalchal* programming. So the journalists came up with another way of keeping Nepalis informed. Since comedy counted as entertainment, and was thus permitted, they asked a well-known comedian to sing the news—in a comedy style, naturally.

As the authorities became increasingly frustrated with the journalists' defiance, they shut down some of the most popular radio stations entirely. Still, however, Nepalis found ways of ensuring that the news got out. In the eastern town of Biratnagar, crowds gathered to hear the news read out by megaphone. When one megaphone broadcaster was arrested, another would pop up in his place.

The determination of ordinary Nepalis to stand up for truth led to a historic retreat by the country's lawless rulers. In 2006, hundreds of thousands swarmed onto the streets of the Nepalese capital, Kathmandu, despite warnings that those trying to enter the city would be shot. Faced with such defiance, the despotic monarch finally agreed to back down. Elections took place in 2008.

The radio stations of Nepal continue to speak out—even, and especially, when the politicians don't like it.

Hot Gossip

When war began in Darfur in western Sudan in 2003, the world's politicians refused to take seriously the massacres committed by government-backed *janjawid* militias there. Even as Sudanese government planes bombed villages and as tens of thousands of civilians were killed, governments were determined to look away.

Eventually, not least because concerned citizens around the world made their voices heard, the killing became impossible to ignore. The UN Security Council authorized

Khartoum, November 2008. A Sudanese journalist gets her message across.

Credit: Ashraf Shazly/AFP/Getty Images

an international peacekeeping force and in 2005 referred the crimes of Darfur to the International Criminal Court. In 2008, the court's prosecutor announced his intention to indict the Sudanese president, Omar al-Bashir. It seemed that "never again" might at last be more than an empty phrase.

And yet, the people for whom the news mattered most

were not allowed to hear the news. Sudanese journalists were forbidden to write about the indictment.

In November 2008, journalists and editors organized unprecedented protests against the curbs on what they could write. Newspapers temporarily closed themselves down in protest against the suppression of free speech. (The regime also closed down newspapers as a punishment for protesting—the same action, for opposite reasons. On the one hand, journalists refused to publish their papers because of censorship. On the other hand, the regime closed papers down that dared to challenge the government.)

When papers resumed publishing, they still faced the challenge of censorship. Journalists at the Khartoum newspaper *Ajrass Al-Hurriya* ("Bells of Freedom") were determined to write about the indictment of President Bashir. They knew that, under ordinary circumstances, such a story could never get past the censor.

They therefore devised a strategy. When the censor arrived at work, staff gathered near the desk where he sat checking the page proofs. They began discussing a mix of tempting gossip and red-hot political stories, in hopes that the censor would be distracted from his work, and fail to read as carefully as he was supposed to.

The censor was duly distracted, and the offending article was published—forbidden themes and all. As one editor at the paper said, "It's a way of hitting back."

5

Foiling Vote Robbers

It's not the voting that's democracy, it's the counting.
—Tom Stoppard, *Jumpers*

Faking It

Slobodan Milošević, Serbia's warmongering leader during the 1990s, was a master of manipulation in the former Yugoslavia. But, as the endgame approached, even Milošević lost his touch.

He and his henchmen had little idea how to cope with the mischievous Otpor ("Resistance"), the student movement that proved more effective in energizing opposition to Milošević than his political foes had ever been. Even as Otpor's members were arrested and beaten, they mocked the authorities. As one of Otpor's leaders pointed out later, the regime found itself in a bind. "I'm full of humor and irony and you are beating me, arresting me," Srdja Popović said in an interview for Steve York's and Peter Ackerman's documentary *Bringing Down a Dictator*. "That's a game you always lose."

In advance of elections in September 2000, the authorities became increasingly enraged at Otpor's success. Police raided the group's offices in the Serb capital, Belgrade, confiscating computers and campaign materials.

Otpor exacted sweet revenge. On phone lines which they knew would be tapped, they discussed how they would receive a large quantity of additional supplies of election stickers and other materials at a certain time on a certain day. They invited news photographers to witness the delivery. Then, at the appointed hour, volunteers began unloading boxes from a truck, staggering toward the Otpor office, apparently weighed down by the weight of all the pamphlets and posters.

The waiting police triumphantly moved in to seize the boxes. As they did so, they realized that the cartons were not heavy at all, but strangely light. They were empty—as empty as the police action itself.

Orders were orders, however. The police could not stop confiscating what they had been ordered to confiscate. Under the mocking eyes of reporters and other onlookers, the police impounded a large quantity of empty cardboard boxes.

It is possible to do magic tricks with some simple photographic software. Crowds can be digitally multiplied in seconds. But

doing so to create the optical illusion of electoral support may be embarrassing if noticed, as this postcard from the run-up to the Serb elections of 2000—headlined "Enough of the Lies!"—clearly shows.

In large part because of the Otpor campaign described above, crowds in support of Slobodan Milošević were, from the regime's point of view, worryingly small as the elections of September 24, 2000 approached—even after the authorities bused in paid extras to beef up the numbers.

The authorities then came up with what probably seemed like a bright idea at the time. With a click of the

Serbia, 2000. Not such a large crowd, after all.

Credit: NUNS/Independent Association of Journalists of Serbia

mouse, crowds can be multiplied as often as you like. Tweaked photographs duly appeared in the pro-Milošević media, showing vast, loyal (and fictional) crowds. On the front page of the progovernment *Večernje Novosti*, the numbers looked large enough that the official claims of a 100,000-strong pro-Milošević crowd seemed credible.

The gimmick backfired, however, when observant Serbs pointed out that many people—including, for example, the snowy-haired man, the young woman with long dark hair, and the gray-haired gent gazing out from the front of the crowd—appeared in the photograph twice. Milošević's critics reprinted the photograph as a popular postcard, noting that the real number who had attended the rally was a mere fifteen thousand. They added circles to emphasize the point.

Ah, said the loyalists sheepishly. It must have been a technical error.

Within twelve days of the stolen elections, Milošević was gone.

Counting the Cost

Again and again there comes a time in history when the person who dares to say that 2 + 2 = 4 is punished with death . . . The question is not one of knowing what punishment or reward attends the making of this calculation. The question is that of knowing whether two and two do make four.

—ALBERT CAMUS, *The Plague*

The rule of Ferdinand Marcos, president of the Philippines for twenty years, was corrupt and brutal. When exiled opposition leader Benigno Aquino returned to his country, he knew the risks he was incurring. "If it's my fate to die by an assassin's bullet, so be it," Aquino told journalists accompanying him on the plane back to the Philippines. He was shot dead upon disembarking at Manila airport on August 21, 1983.

Marcos supporters perhaps hoped Aquino's violent death would create a climate of fear that would quell opposition. Instead, Aquino's widow, Corazon (popularly known as Cory), declared that *she* would run against Marcos in her husband's stead.

Marcos agreed to elections, which were scheduled for February 7, 1986. Marcos was known for stealing elections. There was every reason to believe that he could and would do it again—with the help of violence, if need be.

The action of thirty female computer technicians meant, however, that the regime's attempts to falsify the results were doomed. The women were responsible for tallying the official vote count. When the authorities instructed them to omit numbers that were favorable to the opposition, they walked out of the counting hall in protest at the fraud, noting "discrepancies." They took the computer discs and printouts with them as irrefutable proof of the fraud. In the words of Linda Kapunan, head of the programmers' team, quoted in *People Power: An Eyewitness History*: "There could be attempts to harm our families. But our dignity is not negotiable."

Marcos loyalists insisted that it was much ado about nothing. One general claimed that the computer operators were upset merely because agitators were throwing stones and paper darts. "The women," he said, "have gone for a rest." They would soon be back.

In reality, the women never returned. Instead, they gave a hastily convened press conference in a church and went into hiding from the regime's revenge. As James Fenton noted in his eyewitness account of the fall of Marcos, *The Snap Revolution*, "People had been killed for much, much smaller offenses."

The government claimed that Marcos gained eleven million votes, thus defeating Cory Aquino, who allegedly garnered a mere nine million. But following the programmers' walkout, nobody believed it. The country's bishops praised the women who "refused to degrade themselves by participating in election fraud."

Following the women's walkout, hundreds of thousands of peaceful protesters filled the streets of Manila. They surrounded the tanks and demanded acknowledgment of Aquino's victory.

Marcos assured everybody that he had won, and that he was still in control. He then climbed into an American helicopter and fled with his wife, Imelda, to Hawaii.

The computer programmers came out of hiding. Aquino became the country's president. The women's determination to insist that two plus two can only ever equal four helped change the country.

No, We Didn't!

The regime of Murat Zyazikov—president of the small republic of Ingushetia, neighbor of war-torn Chechnya in southern Russia—has seemed like a bastion of official lawlessness. Human rights organizations—international and Russian alike—documented a pattern of abductions, torture, and killing by security forces there in recent years. But the people of Ingushetia defied Zyazikov, with startling results.

In 2007, few Ingush voters went to the polls, as they were sure the election would be rigged. They felt as though voting could change nothing. How remarkable, then, to find that official returns claimed that an astonishing 98 percent of the 163,000 registered Ingush voters had cast ballots. An overwhelming majority of the votes were allegedly (of course) in favor of the pro-Moscow party and Zyazikov himself.

A challenge to the results seemed unthinkable, especially since Zyazikov had the backing of the Russian leadership. But Zyazikov had not counted on the dogged determination of Ingush citizens.

Protesters launched a campaign. "I Didn't Vote," they declared on a petition of signatures, with accompanying names, addresses, and identity card details. The campaign gained the signatures of more than half of the republic's entire electorate. Ninety thousand voters insisted that they, at least, had never voted. All of which meant that the 98 percent figure was implausible, at best.

Zyazikov declared it was all "real stupidity and nonsense." Those who led the I Didn't Vote campaign were threatened with violence. And still the campaign continued.

Finally, Zyazikov was forced by Moscow to step down in 2008—partly because of the embarrassing lack of legitimacy that the I Didn't Vote campaign revealed. The man of violence lost out to tens of thousands of voters who used nothing but their courage and a few strokes of the pen to help bring him down.

6

Women Say No

Lysistrata: Now tell me, if I have discovered a means of ending the war, will you all second me? . . .

Myrrhine: We will, we will, though we should die of it!

Lysistrata: We must refrain from the male altogether. . . .

Calonice: But if—which the gods forbid—we do refrain altogether from what you say, should we get peace any sooner?

Lysistrata: Of course we should, by the goddesses twain! We need only sit indoors with painted cheeks, and meet our mates lightly clad in transparent gowns of Amorgos silk, and employing all our charms and all our arts; then they will act like mad and they will be wild to lie with us. That will be the time to refuse, and they will hasten to make peace.

—Aristophanes, Lysistrata (411 BCE)

Monrovia, Liberia, 2003. The women were dismissed as crazy. But they succeeded.

White Scarves and Warlords

The history of nonviolent action is not a succession of desperate idealists, occasional martyrs and a few charismatic emancipators. The real story is about common citizens who are drawn into great causes, which are built from the ground up.

—PETER ACKERMAN AND JACK DUVALL, *A Force More Powerful*

The west African nation of Liberia was founded by freed American slaves. The country's coat of arms declares, "The love of liberty brought me here." In the last years of the twentieth century and the early years of the twenty-first century, however, Liberia was anything but a land of liberty. Drug-fueled militias maimed and killed civilians. Government and rebel forces alike raped with impunity. Hundreds of thousands fled. Others were trapped by the unending violence, unable to flee. As one Liberian woman later remembered, "My children had been hungry and afraid for their entire lives."

In spring 2003, a group of women decided to try to end the conflict once and for all. Dressed all in white, hundreds of them sat by the roadside, on the route taken daily by President Charles Taylor, rebel leader–turned–president.

The president's motorcade swept past, slowing down only briefly for a contemptuous glance. But the women returned, day after day. In pouring rain and blazing sunshine alike, they danced and prayed. In the words of Comfort Lamptey, author of a book on the Liberian peace movement of those years, the women were "fighting for the right to be seen, heard, and counted."

Taylor mocked the women for "embarrassing themselves." Still, though, the protests gained momentum. Religious leaders—imams and bishops alike—spoke out in support of the women's demands. Radio stations began reporting sympathetically on the roadside protests. Leymah Gbowee, one of the protest leaders, declared in front of the cameras, "We are tired of our children being raped. We are taking this stand because we believe tomorrow our children will ask us: 'Mama, what was your role during the crisis?'"

Pressed on all sides, Taylor agreed to talk. He met with the women's leaders in the presidential palace. Peace talks with the warring factions began in Ghana a few weeks later.

It soon became clear, however, that the talks were going nowhere. Even as the warlords basked in the comfort of their luxury hotel, they worked the phones, directing a renewed orgy of violence at home in the Liberian capital, Monrovia.

The women decided that enough was enough. Determined to focus on the human cost of the war, they barricaded delegates into the room where the talks were taking place. One of the negotiators, Nigerian General Abdulsalami Abubakar, remembered later: "They said that nobody will come out till that peace agreement was signed." As described in the 2008 documentary film *Pray the Devil Back to Hell*, one warlord tried unsuccessfully to kick his way out of the room. Others tried (and failed) to escape through the windows.

The men with guns agreed to talk seriously at last. A peace deal was struck. Charles Taylor went into exile. International peacekeepers arrived in Monrovia, greeted by cheering crowds. In 2006, Ellen Johnson-Sirleaf became Liberia's peacefully elected president, Africa's first woman leader. Johnson-Sirleaf said: "It was ordinary Liberians who reclaimed the country and demanded peace."

At the time of this writing, Taylor is on trial for crimes against humanity committed in the war in neighboring Sierra Leone.

Abandonment for Peace

Aristophanes never intended the *Lysistrata* story quoted at the opening of this chapter to be taken literally. His play was a satire, a way of pressing for an end to the death and destruction of the long-running Peloponnesian War in Greece in the fifth century BCE. The story played with an obviously unthinkable idea: that women, by withholding their consent to sex, could do something to end a brutal conflict.

Two thousand years later, *Lysistrata* has achieved a real-life momentum of its own, in different contexts around the world.

For example, in 2002, women in southern Sudan acted to stop the twenty-year civil war between the north and the south of the country, in which an estimated two million people had died. Many women in villages affected by the war felt they had no way to influence the debate. But Samira Ahmed, a former university professor, had a plan to give them power. Working with a handful of women from two ethnic groups, she started a practice they called "sexual abandoning." In time, thousands more joined.

"Women decided that by withholding sex from their men they could force them to commit to peace—and it's worked," Ahmed was quoted as saying. In 2005, not least because of all the different grassroots pressures for an end to the war, a peace agreement between north and south was signed.

*
**

The *Lysistrata* tactics had a role to play in Kenya in 2009, too, when many feared a renewal of the postelection violence that had brought the country to the brink of catastrophe a year earlier.

The relationship between the two main political rivals, Prime Minister Raile Odinga and President Mwai Kibaki, remained dangerously tense. Women's groups, fearing a renewed descent into violence, urged the men to settle their differences and, as they put it, "begin to serve the nation they represent." To emphasize the point, they announced a sex strike.

Rukia Subow, chair of one of the groups, argued, "We have seen that sex is the answer. It does not know tribe, it does not have a party, and it happens in the lowest households." Patricia Nyaundi, director of the Federation of Women Lawyers, said the sex strike—limited to one week, for practical reasons—contained a broader Kenyan message: "The idea is to deny ourselves what we consider essential, for the good of our country."

The *Lysistrata*-style strike gained widespread support— even the prime minister's wife, Ida Odinga, declared that she supported it "body and soul."

One man, James Kimondo, told journalists he planned to sue the organizers for what he was forced to endure. Kimondo claimed the sex strike had caused him stress, mental anguish, backache, and lack of sleep.

But women's groups welcomed the success of the action—"Kenyans began talking about issues that are affecting them. And it got the politicians talking." The women even persuaded some sex workers to join the strike.

The sex strike ended with a joint prayer session. The prime minister and the president finally agreed to talk.

*
**

The Colombian city of Pereira was long considered one of the most violent in a violent country. The majority of perpetrators of the city's violence were young men. Much of the violence was gang-related. There were many reasons to join the gang lifestyle, but one of the most compelling was that men believed it made them sexually desirable.

Knowing this, women concluded that sex could hold the key to ending the violence, too.

In 2006, girlfriends and wives of the men of violence refused to engage in any sexual relations in protest against the violence. It became known as the *huelga de piernas cruzadas,* the cross-legged strike.

In the words of Jennifer Bayer, the girlfriend of a gang member, "We want them to know that violence is not sexy."

Ruth Macías, an eighteen-year-old mother of two, told journalists, "This is our way of telling them we don't want to be widows and for our children to grow up without fathers. Until now they didn't want to listen. In this way they will hear us."

The women called for men to turn in their weapons, and recorded a rap song, broadcast on local radio, which sought to bring other women into the campaign: "As women, we are worth a lot . . . We close our legs against the violent men. *Paro sexual!* Sex strike!"

The action of the Pereira women is part of a nationwide pattern, where ordinary Colombians have repeatedly challenged violence—in their neighborhoods, in the workplace, in the countryside. Actions like those of the women of Pereira helped pave the way for action against violence elsewhere.

Ownership

In many countries, women are denied the right to own land or to inherit shared property after a husband's death. In the Ugandan town of Mubende, a recently widowed woman found a way around that problem.

One Sunday morning in early 1996, Noerina Mubiru was confronted by her late husband's relatives as she prepared to leave for church. As described by Aili Mari Tripp in *Women and Politics in Uganda,* ten relatives presented a list of possessions they intended to seize and remove.

The widow had a different thought. Mubiru stripped naked, and walked into the living room where the relatives were gathered. The Ugandan *Daily Monitor* reported that she pointed downwards and declared: "You see, this was one of the properties my husband loved most." Patting her behind, she added: "This was the second item he loved. If anybody wants to remove his property, he will have to start with these and then I can show you the rest."

The father-in-law fainted. The relatives fled.

7

If Not Now, When?

If I am not for myself, who will be for me?
And if I am only for myself, what am I?
And if not now, when?
—Rabbi Hillel the Elder, first century BCE

Shocking Defiance

Disobedience, in the eyes of anyone who has read history, is man's
original virtue. It is through disobedience that progress has been
made, through disobedience and through rebellion.

—OSCAR WILDE

Most of the stories in this book involve a degree of heroism—
unobtrusive or obvious, large or small. Those who committed
these "small acts" have risked harassment, arrest, or even
death. It might seem, then, that the story of Jan Rensaleer
(and others like him) hardly deserves inclusion. Rensaleer,
an industrial engineer, was paid $4 to take part in a research
experiment in New Haven, Connecticut, which ran from
1960 to 1963. The experiment claimed to be about the nature
of memory.

The study, conducted by Stanley Milgram at Yale
University, was in reality designed to test not memory but
obedience. Influenced by the experience of the Holocaust, the
test sought to establish how readily ordinary people might
inflict pain on or even kill a stranger, when ordered to do so.

Participants were divided, apparently at random, into
"teacher" and "learner" (the "learner" was an actor). The
teacher was brought by a staffer to a control panel while the
learner was strapped to a chair in a neighboring room, with
electrodes placed on him. The teacher was to ask questions
of the learner, with each wrong answer resulting in the
teacher administering an electric shock. The shocks allegedly
became stronger with each wrong answer. (In reality, there
was no shock; the learner was an actor, after all.) The lever
administering the shocks had a labeled scale that ran from

"Slight Shock" at 15 volts to "Moderate" to "Danger: Severe Shock" at 375 volts, and finally just "XXX" at 450.

The study proceeded with the learner answering a few questions correctly, but also getting a few of them intentionally wrong. At the 150-volt mark, the actor-learner, following his instructions, begged for the experiment to end and reminded the teacher of his weak heart. If the teacher seemed ready to stop, a laboratory assistant was on hand to encourage him or her to continue. As the simulated shocks escalated, the learner-actor responded accordingly, screaming louder with each increase. In the face of any hesitation, the assistant in a laboratory coat firmly requested that the teacher proceed. At the top end of the shock scale, the "learner" stopped screaming and acted as if he had lost consciousness. Even then, the assistant insisted that the teacher continue to administer shocks, claiming that a nonanswer should be counted as a wrong answer.

The results of the study were remarkable. Almost two-thirds of participants went along with demands to administer electric shocks up to the end of the scale. Many expressed reservations along the way that they were hurting the learner. When told by the staffer that the man was fine, however—or, crucially, that they were not responsible for what happened next—65 percent went ahead as directed. Thus, for example, one woman—confident in her own moral qualities, and representing, in effect, the amoral majority in this experiment—proudly described her character. "I'm unusual; I'm softhearted; I'm a softy." She was also ready to kill, pushing the levers (after some ritual protests) right to the end of the scale. When the unharmed actor walked back into the room, the startled woman was concerned with what *she* had suffered while killing him. "Every time I pressed the button, I died. Did you see me shaking? I was just dying here to think that I was administering shocks to this poor man." She blamed others, and seemed oblivious to what she herself had agreed to do.

Rensaleer, by contrast—by no means unique in the study, but representing a minority of those who took part— took responsibility for his own actions, with important implications, as described by Stanley Milgram himself in his classic account, *Obedience to Authority.*

When he refused to go forward with the shocks, Rensaleer was told by the staffer, "It is absolutely essential that you continue."

"Well, I won't—not with the man screaming to get out," he replied.

"You have no other choice," the staffer said, working off the predetermined script.

"I do have a choice. Why don't I have a choice?" Rensaleer replied. "I came here on my own free will . . . I can't continue, I'm very sorry."

The experiment ended there.

Rensaleer and his fellow refusers did not have to do much. They were told to ask a few questions. They refused requests to press a few levers. And then they went home. They risked nothing—not their jobs, nor even the $4 that the organizers handed over with no strings attached.

And yet, that small act of defiance deserves commemoration, not least because the otherwise unexceptional

Rensaleer and others like him were in a minority. The majority, like the "I'm softhearted" woman, were ready to kill a perfect stranger. Rensaleer and other participants who refused to give lethal shocks when asked to do so proved the exception, not the rule.

We would all like to think that we would repeat Rensaleer's minimal act of resistance. The statistics of the Milgram experiment—including when the experiment was repeated, in other countries around the world—tell a very different story.

In that context, let us hear it for Jan Rensaleer and the minority who were ready to say no. Those who believe in the importance of basic values have saved countless lives—with their actions, or their refusal to take certain actions. The story of Jan Rensaleer reminds us that we can perhaps change more than we ever guessed.

Humiliating Hitler

By early 1943, the Nazis' plan to murder millions of European Jews was moving forward swiftly. The final liquidation of the Warsaw ghetto was only a few months away. One group of Jews in Germany had until that date enjoyed partial protection: those who were married to non-Jews. On February 27, 1943, however, the architects of the Holocaust decided that enough was enough, and began a final sweep to make Berlin free of all Jews, whomever they might be married to. Hitler's powerful and feared propaganda chief, Joseph Goebbels, noted with grim satisfaction in his diary that the endgame had now been reached for the declared goal of a "Jew-free Berlin." He wrote: "They were thrown together in one fell swoop last Sunday and will now be shoved off to the east in short order." The men were held at a Jewish community center in Rosenstrasse in central Berlin, ready for deportation to the camps.

There seemed to be only one way that this story could end—with yet more Nazi bloodshed. Clearly, Hitler's regime was too powerful to be confronted. Instead, what happened next represented one of the most extraordinary and little-told stories of the Second World War.

Hundreds of women began to gather outside the Rosenstrasse deportation point in the days to come, demanding that their husbands be released, and ignoring all threats against them.

Elsa Holzer, whose husband Rudi was held at Rosenstrasse, later described the scene: "As I arrived, I saw a crowd—at six in the morning already! People flowed back and forth. This short little street was black with people. They were like a wave, and they moved like a body, a swaying body." The women chanted: "We want our husbands back!" The Nazis threatened to shoot the women. They only shouted back "Murderers!" and refused to move.

With the Nazis' track record of brutality, the women could reasonably expect to take the lethal threats seriously. On such issues, after all, the Nazis were not known for bluffing. Merely uttering a word of criticism could be fatal, as the courageous students Sophie and Hans Scholl had discovered, executed just a few days earlier for distributing leaflets criticizing Hitler's war.

On this occasion, however, the ending was different. The threats against the women continued. Still, though, they refused to disperse. It was embarrassing for the Nazis to allow the protest in the heart of the German capital to continue. But it was equally embarrassing to beat or kill German women—"our" women—in a public place. After just a few days of these public protests came the astonishing ending.

The men were released. Some were even fetched back from Auschwitz itself, an achievement without parallel. Forty years later, Erich Herzberg, one of those who were saved, described to Nathan Stoltzfus, author of *Resistance of the Heart,* how he and others agreed, as a condition of being released, that he would tell people that conditions in the concentration camp were excellent. Implausibly, Herzberg even insisted, when asked by his Nazi guards, that he and others had suffered no violence. As he put it: "Well, I'm not stupid!"

For decades after the Second World War, the remarkable Rosenstrasse protests and their impact were unknown or ignored. The implications were almost too enormous to grasp, in a context where it was often said that nobody could have protested against Hitler and lived to tell the tale.

The women of Rosenstrasse proved that was not the whole truth. In recent years, they have been publicly honored as never before. In 2003, German director Margarethe von Trotta turned the story of defiance into a film, *Rosenstrasse.* And the story of the protests is now included in the German history curriculum. It is designed to teach the lessons of what nonviolent resistance can achieve even under the most difficult circumstances. Pupils are encouraged to ask: What if millions—not just a few hundred women—had decided to confront the tyrant? How else might history have been changed?

Collective Rescue

It happened so naturally, we can't understand the fuss. I helped simply because they needed to be helped. It's a normal thing to do.

—GEORGETTE BARRAUD, A VILLAGER IN LE CHAMBON

There were countless individual acts of heroism all across Nazi-occupied Europe in the Second World War. In some places, however, bravery involved more than just individuals. Entire communities stood in solidarity with their Jewish neighbors and compatriots, risking their lives to save total strangers.

In Bulgaria, tens of thousands of Jews survived because Bulgarians doggedly refused to follow Nazi orders. The Bulgarian government, which was allied with the Nazis, approved German demands for Jews to be deported to their deaths. But those deportations never took place—because of the many Bulgarians who resisted.

In 1943, arrests were planned, and trains were scheduled for deportations. But dozens of members of parliament signed a petition protesting against the plans. As Dimitar Peshev, organizer of the petition, wrote later: "Jews would be deported and consigned to a fate of which we had only a vague notion but were now beginning to fathom."

Adolf Eichmann, chief scheduler of the deportation trains—the man who prompted Hannah Arendt to coin the term the *banality of evil*—kept demanding that Bulgaria's Jews be deported. The government was eager to do the Nazis' bidding. But ordinary Bulgarians found ways of saying no. Church leaders offered churches and monasteries as places of refuge. They threatened to lie down on the train tracks if need be.

The Bulgarians put two different plans on the table for their Nazi allies. Plan A involved "the deportation of all Bulgarian Jews to Germany's eastern regions for reasons of internal state security" (in other words, certain death). And then—"should the preceding plan prove unfeasible"—there was the milder Plan B, which required the evacuation of tens of thousands of Jews from the Bulgarian capital, Sofia, to the provinces.

To the fury of Eichmann and his colleagues, Plan A indeed proved "unfeasible." Plan B, mere evacuation, was ordered instead. But that caused protests, too. On May 24, 1943, Bulgaria's national holiday became an occasion for popular demonstrations against anti-Jewish policies in Sofia. The head of the Bulgarian Church, Metropolitan Stefan, demonstratively received the country's chief rabbi at his home. In *The Fragility of Goodness*, Tzvetan Todorov quotes the stern telegram that the church leader sent to the Bulgarian king, warning him to protect the country's Jews: "The measure you give will be the measure you get. Know, Boris, that God watches your acts from heaven."

Eventually, the Nazis' Bulgarian allies were forced to explain to Berlin that deportation would "come at too high a political price, both internally and internationally." Grudgingly and astonishingly, the Nazis agreed. Hitler's ambassador to Bulgaria complained to Berlin: "In my meeting yesterday with the prime minister, I have realized that to insist on the deportation at the present time makes no sense whatever." By the end of the year, Jews were granted permission to return to their homes in the capital. None were deported.

As a result of the quiet collective defiance, almost all the Jews in Bulgaria proper—48,000 people, in all—were saved.

In France, in the village of Le Chambon-sur-Lignon, thousands of Jews found safe harbor with the complicity of almost the entire population of Le Chambon and surrounding villages.

The heart of the resistance was the local pastor, André Trocmé. Even as tens of thousands of Jews were rounded up and deported without public protest from Paris in July 1942, Trocmé assailed the failures of France's church leaders, declaring, "The Christian church should drop to its knees and beg pardon of God for its cowardice."

As described in Philip Hallie's *Lest Innocent Blood Be Shed* and in Pierre Sauvage's documentary film *Weapons of the Spirit,* Trocmé and his family were not alone. He worked with thirteen church ministers and their congregations, in and around Le Chambon. Villagers forged identity documents and ration cards, provided education for children, and smuggled people to safety in neighboring Switzerland.

Five thousand lives were saved in this way. Villagers found all of this unremarkable. "How can you call us good?" asked Trocmé's wife, Magda, many years later. "We were doing what had to be done."

In September 1943, the Nazis prepared for the deportation of all Danish Jews to the concentration camps and death. But Georg Duckwitz, a German diplomat with a conscience, deliberately leaked the plans for the roundup, which was due to begin on Rosh Hashanah, the Jewish New Year. Armed with the information from Duckwitz, Danes swung into action.

Teachers fetched children out of class, and told them to go home and pack their things. Friends and strangers alike provided alternative accommodations, so that nobody would be at home when the Nazis came knocking on the door at the registered addresses of Jews. Adults and children checked into hospitals under fictitious names, suffering from fictitious ailments. Others appeared at chapels, as if to attend a funeral. The "mourners"—sometimes hundreds at a time—then traveled at a stately speed out of Copenhagen, as part of a huge, life-giving funeral cortege, as described in Emmy Werner's *A Conspiracy of Decency*. Families were transported to remote beaches, where boats picked them up at night and took them to safety. Others arranged escapes in broad daylight. In Copenhagen, families stepped into canal boats that advertised "Harbor Tours." These special harbor tours avoided traditional sights, delivering their passengers to waiting fishing boats instead. Families hid in the hulls, or were covered by tarpaulins, herrings, and straw, and were ferried to neutral Sweden to wait out the war in safety.

As a result of Duckwitz's whistle-blowing and of Danish solidarity, 99 percent of Denmark's seven thousand Jews survived.

Dangerously Nonviolent

History teaches over and over again that . . . if the nonviolent side can be led to violence, they have lost the argument and they are destroyed.

—MARK KURLANSKY, *Nonviolence: Twenty-five Lessons from the History of a Dangerous Idea*

Perhaps the most famous example of nonviolent resistance is that of Mahatma Gandhi. There are dozens of books, a Hollywood movie, even an opera commemorating his life. The story of the lawyer and barefoot resister who took a twenty-four-day walk to the sea and publicly crumbled a handful of salty mud in defiance of British salt-tax laws is indeed remarkable.

Gandhi's achievements are rightly inscribed in the textbooks. Much less remembered is Gandhi's close friend and ally in the struggle against the British Empire—Pathan (Pashtun) leader Abdul Ghaffar Khan. And yet, Khan's achievements in confronting colonial violence—in what was then northwest India, now Pakistan—were in some ways equally remarkable.

Khan told his followers, "I am going to give you such a weapon that the police and the army will not be able to stand against it . . . That weapon is patience and righteousness." Badshah Khan—literally, "the emperor of Khans"—created an astonishing and powerful Pathan army of nonviolence: the fifty-thousand-strong Servants of God.

Even Gandhi was in awe of the commitment to nonviolence by Khan's Pathan force. Khan biographer Eknath Easwaran quotes Gandhi: "That such men who would have killed a human being with no more thought than they would kill a sheep or a hen should at the bidding of one man have laid down their arms and accepted non-violence as the superior weapon sounds almost like a fairy tale." But, Gandhi concluded, this was real: "Badshah Khan commands willing obedience . . . His non-violence is no lip service. His whole heart is in it."

Khan himself was impatient with those who expressed surprise that a Pathan Muslim might espouse nonviolence.

As he liked to point out: "[Nonviolence] is not a new creed. It was followed 1400 years ago by the Prophet."

As with Gandhi's followers, the determined nonviolence of the Servants of God did not protect them from the violence of the rulers. Khan's arrest in 1930 triggered huge peaceful protests in the city of Peshawar—peaceful protests which were violently suppressed. Colonial troops opened fire and killed more than 200. Soldiers who refused to shoot were themselves jailed.

Khan believed that "all the horrors the British perpetrated on the Pathans had only one purpose: to provoke them to violence." Eventually, the colonial rulers were forced to cede their authority.

The influential and much-jailed Khan remained at odds with Pakistan's post-independence rulers, too. He stayed true to his philosophy of nonviolence until his death in 1988, at the age of 98. Tens of thousands accompanied his coffin across the Khyber Pass, to attend his funeral in Afghanistan.

They Overcame

Each time a person stands up for an ideal, or acts to improve the lot of others, or strikes out against injustice, he sends forth a tiny ripple of hope, and crossing each other from a million different centers of energy and daring, those ripples build a current which can sweep down the mightiest walls of oppression and resistance.
—Robert Kennedy, speaking in South Africa in 1966

The name "Rosa Parks" is rightly famous around the world. Millions know that, on December 1, 1955, the forty-two-

Lincoln Memorial, Washington, D.C., August 28, 1963. They had a dream.
Credit: Bruce Davidson/Magnum

year-old seamstress boarded a bus in Montgomery, Alabama, and took a seat. A few stops later, three white passengers got on. The driver ordered black passengers to vacate their seats. Parks was seated toward the back of the bus, just behind the whites-only section at the front. But a white man did not have a seat, and that was considered unacceptable. The driver asked Parks: "Are you going to stand up?" She said no. When the driver threatened to have her arrested, Parks famously replied, "You may do that."

Parks's arrest sparked a yearlong bus boycott in Montgomery, which played a key role in the civil rights movement. Her act of quiet defiance changed the landscape of America, and she is honored for it. There is a Rosa Parks Museum in Montgomery today.

Much less well known is the story of fifteen-year-old Claudette Colvin. While riding a bus in Montgomery, Colvin refused to give up her seat for a white passenger, and was thrown off and arrested for her peaceful protest in almost identical circumstances. Her protest took place on March 2, 1955—nine months before Rosa Parks's own.

Decades later, Colvin recalled: "We had been studying the Constitution in class. I knew I had rights . . . I was thinking: Why should I have to get up just because a driver tells me to, or just because I'm black?"

Colvin had been stirred by the inspiring lessons of women like Harriet Tubman and Sojourner Truth, who fought against slavery a century earlier. She could not get these figures out of her mind when the bus driver ordered her to give up her seat to a white woman. "My head was just too full of black history, you know, the oppression that we went through. It felt like Sojourner Truth was on one side pushing me down, and Harriet Tubman was on the other side of me pushing me down. I couldn't get up," she later said.

Colvin became a key witness in the court challenge that went to the Federal District Court of Alabama and then the U.S. Supreme Court, thus outlawing segregation on the buses forever. For Colvin, the courtroom appearance was daunting. She told Phillip Hoose, author of *Claudette Colvin: Twice Towards Justice*: "Sometimes I would imagine, 'Claudette, you're a Christian, and you're about to get thrown to the lions and you have one speech to give to the Senate.' In my imagination that courtroom seemed like the

Colosseum, and it felt like I had one last speech. I was going to make the most of it."

And so she did. On November 13, 1956, the U.S. Supreme Court—in a case in which Rosa Parks was personally uninvolved—affirmed that bus segregation was illegal. Montgomery preacher Martin Luther King Jr. declared Colvin a "brave young lady" for her defiance and testimony.

And yet, Colvin has been largely written out of history. She came from the wrong part of town. She had become pregnant by an older man ("statutory rape," she said later) and was thus an unmarried teenage mother. The straight-A student—quiet, well-mannered, devout—wrongly began to be described as a mere teenage troublemaker. Her courage was ignored and forgotten.

Rosa Parks became famous as the woman whose case triggered the Montgomery bus boycott and thus changed history. Colvin, despite her historic role, did not.

Colvin worked for decades as a nursing assistant in the Bronx. In recent years, she has been publicly honored for the first time. In 2005, half a century after her act of defiance, she was invited back to speak at her old school in Montgomery.

For Colvin, the issues revolving around her decision to stay seated were simple. She felt that it was essential not just to worry about injustice, but to confront it head-on. In a conversation with Phillip Hoose, she described her mind-set at that time: "As a teenager, I kept thinking, Why don't the adults around here just *say* something?" she said. "You can't sugarcoat it. You have to take a stand and say, 'This is not right.'"

*
**

Under a government which imprisons unjustly, the true place for a just man is also a prison.

— Henry David Thoreau, *Civil Disobedience* (1849)

Jim Lawson, a preacher who had studied the Gandhian principles of nonviolence in India, met with Martin Luther King Jr. in 1956 at the theological seminary in Oberlin, Ohio. King had gained national fame through the bus boycott in Montgomery that was now under way. Both men were twenty-eight. King was excited by Lawson's stories of his work on nonviolence and insisted that Lawson go to work in the South. "Come as quickly as you can," King urged him. "We really need you."

So Lawson went to Nashville and organized a series of Gandhian workshops there. Over and over again, he and his students, black and white alike, practiced the art of being beaten and insulted, refusing to be provoked. The endlessly repeated role-plays laid the foundation for previously unthinkable victories of nonviolence over violence—just as Gandhi's own victories had done a quarter of a century earlier. Lawson was in search of a simple, obvious injustice that could be challenged—an American equivalent of Gandhi's colonial salt laws. He and his students decided to confront the whites-only lunch counters in Nashville's downtown stores.

Blacks were allowed to spend money in the Nashville stores. They were prohibited, however, from using the toilets or sitting at lunch counters to eat. Lawson and his colleagues decided that must change. A few months later, they began the actions that changed history.

On Saturday February 27, 1960, groups of neatly dressed students sat down at lunch counters all across Nashville. Some were arrested, some were beaten to the ground—just what they had expected and practiced for. John Lewis, a twenty-year-old seminary student from rural Alabama and one of the organizers of the food-counter protests, remembered the mass arrests as a personal turning point. "I felt high, almost giddy with joy," Lewis wrote in his memoir, *Walking with the Wind.* "We sang as we were led into cells much too small for our numbers, which would total eighty-two by the end of the day." The police could hardly keep up with the waves of students who replaced one another at the lunch counters. No sooner was one group arrested than another would politely take its place.

Ten weeks of peaceful protests were accompanied by arrests and increasing violence by those who wanted segregation to continue. Finally, however, the mayor of Nashville was obliged to concede that food counters should be desegregated. On May 10, 1960, the targeted Nashville stores served black customers for the first time in the city's history.

Massive stubbornness can have powerful political consequences.
—GENE SHARP, *Waging Nonviolent Struggle*

Seven months after the desegregation of the Nashville food counters, the U.S. Supreme Court ruled in December 1960 against segregated facilities—including whites-only restaurants and waiting rooms—in interstate bus stations. But the court ruling had little impact on the ground. A mixed group of black and white passengers, mostly students, sought to change that.

The Freedom Riders left Washington, D.C. on May 4, 1961, intending to challenge segregated facilities all across the South. Initially, things seemed easy. On the first part of their journey, there was no violence. But that did not last for long. In South Carolina, John Lewis, veteran of the food-counter protests, was among those who were badly beaten. In Alabama, with the help of local police, a crowd surrounded and set fire to the bus, with chants of "Fry the goddamn niggers!" The Freedom Riders remained determined. They wrote their wills—and continued the journey, even as officials encouraged the Ku Klux Klan to do its worst. In Birmingham, Alabama, Tom Cook, a senior aide to the city police chief, Bull Connor, told Ku Klux Klan leaders (according to an FBI informer in the room, as described in David Halberstam's *The Children*): "You can beat 'em, bomb 'em, maim 'em, kill 'em. I don't give a shit. There will be no, absolutely no arrests."

The violence against the protesters, splashed across the front pages and on the television evening news, awakened millions to the racist reality and to the importance of the protests. Dozens were jailed in the notorious Parchman Farm penitentiary in Mississippi. Meanwhile, however, more and more Freedom Riders continued to arrive on buses from the North. Week after week, the South was flooded with buses filled with black and white passengers, breaking down the walls of segregation.

More than three hundred Freedom Riders were jailed that summer, a quarter of them women. Attorney General Robert Kennedy asked protesters for a cooling-off period. James Farmer, one of the organizers, responded: "We've been cooling off for a hundred years. If we get any cooler, we'll be in a deep freeze."

On July 7, 1961, the growing pressure meant that Lewis and others were released from Parchman jail. (They all refused bail, as a matter of principle. They had, after all, done nothing wrong.) Two months later, the U.S. government enforced the desegregation of bus terminals for the first time.

In the years to come, the victories of nonviolence against officially sponsored violence continued. Many argued that the small cumulative changes were trivial or meaningless when seen in the larger context. Martin Luther King Jr. disagreed. He echoed a prediction by Robert Kennedy when he told a BBC interviewer in 1964, "I am very optimistic about the future . . . I have seen certain changes in the United States in the past few years that have surprised me. I believe we may be able to get a Negro president in less than forty years."

Few believed him.

Then, on January 20, 2009, sixty-nine-year-old Congressman John Lewis, representative since 1987 of Georgia's fifth political district, was invited to attend a luncheon to mark that day's presidential inauguration. David Remnick described in the *New Yorker* how Lewis received an autographed photograph with a simple message that harkened back half a century to the defiant, choreographed arrests in the Nashville stores, and the murderous beatings in Alabama: "Because of you, John," the dedication said. It was signed: "Barack Obama."

Unstoppable Spring

I believe that unarmed truth and unconditional love will have the final word in reality. That is why right, temporarily defeated, is stronger than evil triumphant.

—Martin Luther King Jr., quoted by
Malalai Joya in her memoir *Raising My Voice*

Under the strict rule of the Taliban between 1996 and 2001, a range of innocuous and popular Afghan pastimes, from kite-flying to chess, were banned. The punishment for breaking the myriad rules of the Taliban included mutilation and public execution. Education was denied to women and girls; the all-enveloping burqa, covering a woman from head to toe, was compulsory throughout Afghanistan. Even women's laughter was banned.

The apparent defeat of the Taliban regime in 2001 did not usher in a brave new world where the voices of ordinary people were listened to, and where a woman's voice could be respected. In many parts of the country, warlords with murderous track records remained in power.

All the more dramatic, then, was the sudden appearance of an unknown young woman who on December 17, 2003 demanded the right to speak at the *loya jirga*, the constitutional assembly in the Afghan capital, Kabul. "I would like to say a few words, Mr. Chairman!" she piped up. "We kids can't get a word in!"

The chairman asked for calm and explained to the hundreds of delegates that the girl had traveled far. He gave her the floor for three minutes.

The twenty-five-year-old woman took her place in front

of a microphone on the floor of the assembly and looked out at the room of turbaned, bearded men from across Afghanistan— including battle-hardened warlords who had fought foreign armies and terrified those who would oppose them. Many had guns by their side. The woman began to speak.

"My name is Malalai Joya from Farah province," she began simply. And then, adjusting her black headscarf, she held the microphone stand with one hand and delivered the kind of truths no one expected to hear from her, or from anybody else.

"I wish to criticize my compatriots in this room," she said. "Why would you allow criminals to be present at this *loya jirga*—warlords responsible for our country's situation?" A few delegates applauded, while others sat stone-faced. Joya continued: "They oppress women and have ruined our country. They should be prosecuted. They might be forgiven by the Afghan people—but not by history."

There was an uproar. Delegates jumped to their feet, waving their hands in the air. The chairman shouted, "Sit down! The sister has crossed the line of what is considered common courtesy.... She is banished from this assembly and cannot return. Send her out. Guards, throw her out!"

Malalai Joya's speech, which can be watched on YouTube, endeared her to ordinary Afghans even as it infuriated the warlords. There were immediate death threats—and a massive popular reception in her hometown. She herself wrote later: "For me, telling truth was not a choice. I did not want fame or special recognition, but had to speak out." She was elected to the Afghan parliament with huge support in 2005.

For some, her outspokenness remained a threat. In 2007, she was suspended from parliament because of her criticisms.

She remains unbowed, despite five assassination attempts. "They will not kill my voice, because it will be the voice of all Afghan women," she said. "You can cut the flower—but you cannot stop the coming of spring."

Finding Humanity

Nonviolent Palestinian resistance in the occupied territories has often unsettled and enraged the Israeli authorities even more than violent resistance, which is in some ways simpler to confront.

The first, largely nonviolent *intifada* (uprising; literally, "shaking off") lasted from 1987 to 1993. In 1989, the villagers of Beit Sahour, near Bethlehem in the Israeli-occupied West Bank, organized a nonviolent protest, insisting: "No taxation without representation." The organizers of the protest declared: "The military authorities do not represent us, and we did not invite them to come to our land. Must we pay for the bullets that kill our children?" They believed the answer was no—and organized a tax strike accordingly.

Punishment was swift. There were beatings and arrests. The Israeli authorities imposed a curfew and cut the phone lines. No food was allowed into Beit Sahour. Journalists, diplomats, and sympathetic Israelis alike were prevented from entering the town. The military ransacked stores and seized property with a far greater value than the taxes withheld. The siege of the town lasted from September 22 through October 31, 1989. As Roger Cohen noted in the *New York Times*, "Israel complains, rightly, when Palestinians use violence. Beit Sahour has chosen a totally nonviolent means of protest, and Israel is using force to crush it."

A draft resolution at the United Nations Security Council criticized the Israeli siege and the subsequent suffering endured by ordinary Palestinians. Fourteen members of the Security Council voted in favor. Only one government voted against. The United States vetoed the resolution—thus blocking support for nonviolent protest against a government's illegal actions and sending a message that reverberated down the years.

General, your tank is a powerful vehicle.
It smashes down forests and crushes a hundred men.
But it has one defect:
It needs a driver.

—BERTOLT BRECHT

Yigal Bronner, a former member of the Israel Defense Forces, included the above quotation in an open letter he wrote in 2002. He and hundreds of others refused to serve with the Israeli army in the occupied territories. These soldiers were from prestigious elite units, who had seen active combat and risked their lives. Many were jailed for their refusal to serve in the occupied territorities. They became known as *seruvniks* from the Hebrew word *seruv*—refusal.

The *seruvniks* drew their compatriots' and the world's attention to the dehumanizing effects of the occupation on both Israelis and the three million Palestinians in the occupied territories. They insisted, in what became known as the Combatants' Letter: "We shall not continue to fight beyond the 1967 borders in order to dominate, expel, starve, and humiliate an entire people. We hereby declare that we shall continue serving in the Israel Defense Forces in any mission that serves Israel's defense. The missions of occupation and oppression do not serve this purpose—and we shall take no part in them."

Bronner's letter to the general who called him to serve in the occupied territories was a meditation on the relationship between an individual soldier and the army that orders him to do the unthinkable. Bronner had one such experience when he, working as a tank gunner, was ordered to fire a missile into a group of people. "I am the final small cog in the wheel of this sophisticated war machine. I am the last and smallest link in the chain of command. I am supposed to simply follow orders—to reduce myself to stimulus and response. To hear the command 'Fire!' and pull the trigger, to bring the overall plan to completion," Bronner wrote. "And I am supposed to do all this with the natural simplicity of a robot, who senses nothing beyond the shaking of the tank as the shell is ejected from the gun barrel and flies to its target."

Bronner wrote that, although he was not a particularly gifted soldier, he was capable of thinking. And so he refused to fire. He acknowledged that he was "a buzzing gnat that you will swat and try to crush before striding on." But his warning to the general and Israel's political leaders was powerful: "One single gnat can't halt a tank, certainly not a column of tanks, certainly not the entire march of folly. But . . . ultimately other gunners, drivers, and commanders, who will see more and more aimless killing, will also start thinking and buzzing. There are already many hundreds of us. Ultimately, our buzzing will turn into a deafening roar, a roar that will echo in your ears and in those of your children. Our protest will be recorded in the history books, for all generations to see. So, general, before you swipe me away, perhaps you too should do a little thinking."

Refusing to participate, as the *seruvniks* did, is one way of drawing attention to abuses and crimes. Another is simply to speak out about what one has seen or done. A group called Breaking the Silence, organized by former Israeli soldiers since 2004, collects soldiers' personal testimonies. By encouraging soldiers to speak out and by providing an outlet for their testimonies, it has weakened the culture of denial— thus bolstering the courage of those who understand the need for the truth.

The Israeli government insisted that it did not violate the laws of war when twelve hundred Palestinians, mostly civilians, died in the space of just a few weeks during the Cast Lead operation in Gaza in December 2008 and January 2009 (the Palestinian group Hamas fired rockets into civilian areas in Israel at the same time, resulting in thirteen deaths).

Others disagreed with the official Israeli version. In the context of a war, it always requires courage to speak out. As Susan Sontag noted in *Refusenik! Israel's Soldiers of Conscience*, in 2004: "It will always be unpopular—it will always be deemed unpatriotic—to say that the lives of the members of the other tribe are as valuable as one's own."

Despite that, some Israeli soldiers were ready to speak out about abuses that they had witnessed or committed during the Cast Lead operation. Breaking the Silence collected and published dozens of powerful testimonies. The publication infuriated the government—and helped act as a wake-up call for others who were ready to confront the truth about the lives lost because of what a UN inquiry found to be Israel's "indiscriminate attacks" and "deliberate attacks against the civilian population" in Gaza (including shooting those who carried white flags).

In the words of one soldier, describing to Breaking the Silence his part in the military operation in Gaza: "You feel like a child playing around with a magnifying glass, burning up ants. Really. A twenty-year-old kid should not have to do these kinds of things to other people."

8

Revealing Secrets

Where is there dignity unless there is honesty?

—Cicero

Truth is like the sun.
You can shut it out for a time,
but it ain't goin' away.

—Elvis Presley

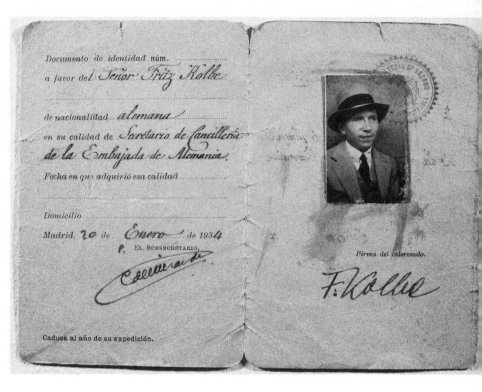

Fritz Kolbe risked his life to share information that helped defeat Hitler.
Long after his death, his courage was finally recognized.

Too Brave

Fritz Kolbe, an unassuming junior German diplomat who loathed the Nazis, repeatedly risked his life to smuggle Hitler's most important secrets into the hands of the Allies. His courageous actions helped change the course of the Second World War. And yet, after 1945 he was treated as a pariah, ignored or simply forgotten. Only in recent years has that finally begun to change.

The story begins in 1935, when Kolbe was working at the German consulate in Madrid. Ernst Kochertaler, a German-Jewish businessman, came to the consulate to renounce his German citizenship in protest against Hitler's new anti-Jewish laws. Even during their brief first official meeting, Kochertaler noticed Kolbe's obvious lack of enthusiasm for the Nazi cause. Intrigued, he invited Kolbe for coffee shortly afterwards. The two men became friends. Kochertaler told Kolbe, "You are the only German I want to talk to now."

Kolbe was posted to South Africa, and Kochertaler moved to Switzerland. When Kolbe returned to Berlin at the beginning of the Second World War in 1939, he was initially assigned routine clerical work. Gradually, however, his work gave him access to increasingly sensitive information about the regime. He traveled to Hitler's headquarters in the East, and was horrified by what he learned about the Nazi murder machine.

In 1943, he succeeded—not least through judicious chatting up of a woman he met in an elite bomb shelter—in being selected as a diplomatic courier, hand-carrying official Nazi documents to the German Embassy in neutral

Switzerland. For Kolbe, it was the perfect assignment. Along with his official papers, he carried unofficial cargo. Hidden under his baggy trousers were secret documents that he had collected for months. The documents were wrapped around his legs with string.

Through his friend Kochertaler, Kolbe approached British diplomats in the Swiss capital, Bern. The British refused to meet him. They concluded that since Kolbe wanted no money, he must obviously be a fake.

Allen Dulles, U.S. intelligence station chief in Switzerland and later head of the CIA, was also cautious. But he remembered how, twenty-six years earlier, he had turned down a request to meet with a Russian radical because he had a more important appointment—a game of tennis. He thus missed the chance to meet Vladimir Lenin, who shortly afterwards went home and led the Russian Revolution in 1917. Dulles decided that on this occasion he should meet with the mystery guest, just in case.

Kolbe kept producing one document after another—"like a magician pulling dozens of surprises out of his sleeve," according to Lucas Delattre in his biography of Kolbe, *Spy at the Heart of the Third Reich*. Kolbe refused to accept money, saying only: "My wish is to shorten the war." In the next two years, Kolbe repeatedly smuggled top-secret documents to the Allies, at enormous personal risk. (In case his night-time absences from the Swiss hotel were noticed, his cover story was that he was fond of visiting brothels. He visited a doctor for a checkup for sexually transmitted diseases and kept the bill as supporting evidence.)

His flow of information—2,600 documents in all—was, in the words of Richard Helms of the CIA, "the most important information ever supplied by an agent working for the Allies." Allen Dulles reckoned Kolbe to be "one of the outstanding intelligence sources of the war."

All of which might suggest that Kolbe would become an acclaimed hero after 1945. Instead, the German government refused to let him work as a diplomat, arguing that he had "betrayed his country." Others thought his track record looked suspiciously clean, and that, therefore, something must be wrong. The American government, meanwhile, was more interested in bringing Nazi scientists to work in the United States than in helping an unassuming idealist who was no longer needed.

Kolbe moved to Switzerland and became a chainsaw salesman there. He died in obscurity in 1971.

More than thirty years after his death, a room was named after him in the German foreign ministry—the same ministry that refused to reemploy him because he was a "traitor." As foreign minister Joschka Fischer noted, with some understatement: "It was not a glorious page in our foreign ministry's history."

Peter Sichel, who in 1945 was chief of the Berlin bureau of the Office of Strategic Services (later the CIA), paid tribute to Kolbe six decades later: "Like most great men, he was rather simple. He knew what he had to do and did not give it a second thought."

Insecurity Council

No one else—including myself—has ever done what Katharine Gun did: tell secret truths at personal risk, before an imminent war, in time, possibly, to avert it. Hers was the most important and courageous leak I've ever seen, more timely and potentially more effective than the Pentagon Papers.

—DANIEL ELLSBERG

Katharine Gun was a twenty-eight-year-old translator of Mandarin Chinese at Britain's Government Communications Headquarters. On January 31, 2003, she went to work as usual. She bought a coffee and a cinnamon roll, took it upstairs, and sat down at her desk. What she read when she turned on her computer changed her life forever.

An e-mail in her inbox was from Frank Koza, "head of regional targets" at GCHQ's American equivalent, the National Security Agency in Fort Meade, Maryland. Koza asked Gun and her colleagues to eavesdrop on discussions by key Security Council governments, including allies, tapping both their work and home phones. The information gathered could provide leverage to help the U.S. government and its British allies persuade reluctant governments to agree to the planned invasion of Iraq.

Gun's daily work involved eavesdropping. She was paid to listen to other people's private conversations. But Gun had always believed her job was to gather information about those who posed a danger to the security of the UK and its allies. She never expected to spy on democratic members of the Security Council like France, Chile, and Mexico, whose only crime was to feel queasy about President George W. Bush's proposed war.

Gun was especially unhappy, given that she and her colleagues had received an official e-mail just a week earlier, reassuring GCHQ staff that they would never be asked to do anything illegal. "I know from the questions you have asked," the e-mail said, "that some of you have concerns about the legal or ethical basis of war against Iraq—if and when it happens—and GCHQ's part in it. Well, there is no question of any member of GCHQ being asked to do anything which is not lawful."

At the time, the e-mail (quoted in Marcia and Thomas Mitchell's *The Spy Who Tried to Stop a War*) seemed like a relief. But the Koza e-mail now in Gun's inbox bluntly contradicted that comforting message. After a few days' agonizing, Gun gave Koza's e-mail to a friend, who in turn handed it to the *Observer* in London. The newspaper hesitated to publish it. Editors worried that the astonishing e-mail might be fake, a deliberate setup. After all, could any government be so shameless in its determination to start a war?

The answer, it seemed, was yes. The *Observer*'s Washington correspondent rang the switchboard of the National Security Agency and asked to be put through to Koza. Briefly—until Koza's secretary understood, too late, who the call was from—Koza's existence was admitted to be real. The conversation went like this:

"Frank Koza's office."

"May I speak to Frank Koza, please?"

"Who may I say is calling?"

"Ed Vulliamy of the *Observer* newspaper in London."

[Pause.]

"Who do you want to speak to?"

"Frank Koza."

"Sorry, I've never heard of him."

The *Observer*'s story made headlines around the world. It triggered angry reactions, including some from the planned spying targets. Chileans, for example, understandably believed that the end of the Pinochet era fifteen years earlier meant that their country would no longer be the victim of U.S. dirty tricks. The Americans'

newly revealed eavesdropping scheme suggested that was not the case.

In the UK, an investigation into the leak was launched. Gun was arrested and charged with breaching the Official Secrets Act. She seemed certain to be jailed. Then, just as the trial opened a year later in 2004, the prosecution announced that it would be offering no evidence. The case collapsed, like a house of cards.

The prosecution was apparently confronted with the absurdity of its own position—seeking to prosecute somebody for highlighting actions intended to pave the way for a war that many, including UN Secretary-General Kofi Annan, regarded as illegal.

The Crown Prosecution Service said it had too little evidence to convict Gun, because of "the prosecution's inability . . . to disprove the defence of necessity." In plain English: A jury could be expected to conclude that Gun had done the brave and decent thing. Twelve free men and women might agree with her conclusion that "[t]his needed to get out." In short, they might conclude that the British and U.S. governments were more culpable than Gun herself.

Frank Koza's reaction to the whole affair remains unrecorded. But Koza was not the only one who kept quiet. Gun's readiness to risk a long jail sentence for exposing the truth about U.S. government lawlessness was treated as essentially irrelevant, in the country where that lawlessness most urgently needed to be addressed.

The U.S. media remained silent on the case, until editors received a wake-up kick from outside. When the actor Sean Penn and others publicly highlighted Gun's case (Penn described her as a "hero of the human spirit"), previously bored editors briefly decided that such jail-defying courage, in connection with illegal actions by the United States, might actually be of marginal interest to their readers and audience, after all.

Gun remains matter-of-fact about the whole incident. "It cost me my job. That is it, basically," she says. "I do not have any regrets."

Ugly Scenes

Some whistle-blowers are commemorated in the history books. Ron Ridenhour, who drew attention to the My Lai massacre of hundreds of civilians in Vietnam in March 1968, is justly remembered. So, too, is Daniel Ellsberg, whose leak of the Pentagon Papers in 1971 hastened the end of the Vietnam War.

Other whistle-blowers have been less honored, even when the impact of their action is substantial. Take the case of Joseph Darby, a loyal soldier stationed with the U.S. forces in Iraq.

One day in January 2004, Darby was shown disturbing photographs of U.S. soldiers abusing detainees at Abu Ghraib jail in Baghdad. Darby informed his superiors about the photographs. He was promised anonymity, in case he suffered retribution for his honesty.

At first, nothing happened. But when the photographs were leaked a few months later, they became front-page news and shocked millions around the world.

U.S. Defense Secretary Donald Rumsfeld provided the opposite of the promised anonymity. On May 7, 2004, Darby was sitting with hundreds of fellow soldiers in a crowded mess hall in Baghdad, watching the television news. Suddenly, Rumsfeld named Darby as the man who revealed what had happened at Abu Ghraib.

Darby described in an interview with the BBC what happened next: "I was sitting midbite when he said it, and I was like, 'Oh, my God.' And the guys at the table just stopped eating and looked at me." Those sitting with him knew immediately that the implications of Rumsfeld's words were serious. "Darb," said one, "We've got to move."

As it turned out, Darby's fellow soldiers were mostly friendly. Many shook his hand to commend him for his honesty. In his hometown of Corriganville, Maryland, by contrast, there was deep hostility. Darby's revelations of wrongdoing by U.S. forces made him a "rat," a "traitor," a "no-good." Darby's wife Bernadette reported, "People were mean. They were saying he was a walking dead man, he was walking around with a bull's-eye on his head." Darby and his family were told that they must move, for their own safety.

Millions of words have been written about the Abu Ghraib photographs, and about the "gloves-off" policy of the Bush government which allowed the horrific abuses to take place. Perhaps the history books will give Joseph Darby more credit for his courage in exposing those abuses than he has received so far.

9

Personal Lives, Public Impact

To see a world in a grain of sand

—William Blake

A Love Supreme

In the early hours of July 11, 1958, in the tiny community of Central Point, Virginia, the county sheriff, his deputy, and the jailer—a group that made up the entire law enforcement establishment of Caroline County—marched into the unlocked home of Mildred and Richard Loving. Once inside, they entered the downstairs bedroom and shone flashlights into the faces of the newlyweds.

The sheriff demanded that Richard, startled from sleep, explain what he was doing in bed with "that woman." While Richard did not immediately answer, Mildred explained, "I'm his wife." Richard then pointed to the marriage certificate hanging on the wall. The sheriff retorted, "That's no good here!" The Lovings, married just a few weeks earlier, were taken to the local jail.

The Lovings had been childhood sweethearts. When Mildred became pregnant, she and Richard traveled to Washington, D.C. and quietly married there. By traveling out of Virginia, they thought they had avoided the ban on interracial marriage—*miscegenation,* to use the official, ugly term—that existed in Virginia and in many other states across America. They were wrong. They were charged with "unlawfully and feloniously" leaving Virginia to get married, and with illegal cohabitation.

The Lovings were sentenced to one year in prison, suspended on condition that they leave the state and never return as a couple. They moved to Washington (which Mildred Loving hated). Occasionally they visited their friends and family back in Virginia—but they were only allowed to do so separately.

Still, though, the couple remained unhappy at what they saw as the court's denial of their rights. Five years after the original conviction, Mildred wrote to Attorney General Robert Kennedy, asking for his help. Her request was simple: that she and her husband be allowed to visit their families in Virginia together.

With the help of the American Civil Liberties Union, the Lovings appealed to the Virginia courts. Turning down their appeal in January 1965, Judge Leon Bazile explained that the ban on mixed marriage was God's idea of a well-ordered world. Phyl Newbeck's account of the case, *Virginia Hasn't Always Been for Lovers,* quotes the written judgment: "Almighty God created the races white, black, yellow, malay and red, and he placed them on separate continents. And but for the interference with his arrangement there would be no cause for such marriages. The fact that he separated the races shows that he did not intend for the races to mix." By falling and remaining in love, in other words, the Lovings were deemed to have proved their ungodliness.

The Lovings appealed again, this time to the U.S. Supreme Court. Richard Loving went to the heart of the matter: "I love my wife—and it is just unfair that I can't live with her in Virginia." Finally, the judges agreed. On June 6, 1967 the Supreme Court overturned the Lovings' conviction—thus also overturning the bans on interracial marriage that still existed in many U.S. states.

The justices reached a simple, unanimous conclusion: "The freedom to marry has long been recognized as one of the vital personal rights essential to the orderly pursuit of happiness by free men . . . These convictions must be reversed. It is so ordered."

The Lovings returned home to Central Point, where they lived out the rest of their lives. Richard died in a car accident in 1975, just eight years after the court decision; Mildred lost an eye in the same crash. She raised her family, attended church, and remained largely out of the public arena for decades.

*
* *

In June 2007, on the fortieth anniversary of the Supreme Court ruling, Mildred Loving made a new public statement of her own—this time, on behalf of those who are forbidden to marry because of a different kind of prejudice. Her testimony in favor of same-sex marriage drew directly on her own experience:

> My generation was bitterly divided over something that should have been so clear and right. The majority believed what the judge said, that it was God's plan to keep people apart, and that government should discriminate against people in love. But I have lived long enough now to see big changes . . .

> Surrounded as I am now by wonderful children and grandchildren, not a day goes by that I don't think of Richard and our love, our right to marry, and how much it meant to me to have that freedom to marry the person precious to me, even if others thought he was the "wrong kind of person" for me to marry.

> I believe all Americans, no matter their race, no matter their sex, no matter their sexual orientation, should have that same

freedom to marry . . . I support the freedom to marry for all. That's what Loving, and loving, are all about.

Mildred Loving died in May 2008, at age sixty-eight. Six months later, Barack Obama was voted into the White House. When the forty-fourth president of the United States was born in 1961, the "miscegenation" of his Kansan mother and his Kenyan father was illegal in more than half of America's states. Mildred and Richard Loving changed that.

Going Dutch

In 1994, when Boris Dittrich, a thirty-nine-year-old Dutch judge and one of the first openly gay members of the country's parliament, began arguing in favor of marriage for same-sex couples, resistance to the idea was almost universal. In a time before the subject of gay marriage had been broached in many countries, not only did traditionalists oppose the idea, but many gays and lesbians complained that this was merely copying a heterosexual lifestyle. The Dutch prime minister, Wim Kok, also rebuked Dittrich for his outlandish idea, telling him, "We don't want to seem like the world's nutcase."

But Dittrich persisted.

In 1998, Dittrich's party held the balance of power in forming a new government. Dittrich and his party insisted that the government had to agree to support same-sex marriage to get Dittrich's party to form a successful ruling coalition. Only if the majority partners in the coalition accepted Dittrich's proposal for the legalization of gay marriage would his smaller party join the government. Faced with the prospect of power slipping away, the prospective coalition partners felt obliged to support Dittrich. Same-sex marriage became legal in the Netherlands three years later, in 2001.

The decision in the Netherlands paved the way for change in other countries. In 2003, Belgium followed the Dutch lead. A clutch of other countries, from Spain to South Africa, adopted similar laws in quick succession. At the time of this writing, same-sex marriage has been legalized in five U.S. states. That number seems certain to grow.

Dittrich married his partner of twenty-four years, artist Jehoshua Rozenman, in 2006. He was knighted by Queen Beatrix of the Netherlands in the same year for his contribution to politics. He now works for Human Rights Watch in New York, advocating for improved gay rights around the world.

The institution of same-sex marriage is increasingly taken for granted in those places where it has been made legal. And all because one country dared to be "the world's nutcase."

Trouser Power

Sudanese journalist Lubna Hussein was charged in July 2009 under Article 152 of Sudan's criminal code, banning "indecent clothing in public." What was the offense? While sitting with a group of women friends in a café, she had been wearing a pair of slacks.

The twelve other women who were sitting with her and who were charged together with Hussein all pleaded guilty. They were punished with ten lashes and a fine. Hussein insisted, however, that she had done nothing wrong and challenged the government to do its worst.

As a public information officer working for the United Nations, Hussein could have claimed immunity from prosecution. Instead, she resigned her job to fight the case—"so that I could face the Sudanese authorities and make them show to the world what they consider justice to be," she said. She even sent hundreds of invitations to journalists and others to witness her public flogging, should it come to that.

The Sudanese government, embarrassed by the growing publicity for the case, twice postponed the trial. When the case finally came to court, the perplexed judge asked Hussein to consider immunity. She again refused.

Her own lawyer suggested that she agree to pay the $200 fine that was imposed on her. (The government did not want to add to its own woes by giving her a flogging and was ready to let her off with a fine.) Hussein refused to pay for a crime she felt she had not committed. She would rather go to jail. (Which, briefly, she did.)

In Hussein's words: "I am Muslim. I understand Muslim law. But I ask: What passage in the Koran says women can't wear pants?"

Hussein herself never wavered in her beliefs, as she showed with her defiant choice of outfit on the day of her sentencing. She turned up wearing the same "indecent" trousers that had led to her arrest in the first place.

Hussein said she was thinking not just of herself but also of her own young daughters and their future. "I pray that the next generation will see we had the courage to fight for their future before it was too late."

Paper, Hair, and Lipstick

Achieving or maintaining normality can sometimes be the most remarkable achievement of all. More than 10,000 civilians were killed during the three-year siege of the Bosnian capital, Sarajevo, between 1992 and 1995 (100,000 died in all of Bosnia). Sarajevans daily ran the gauntlet of Bosnian Serb snipers as they went out of their homes to fetch a bucket of water or a loaf of bread.

Shells rained down on the city—including on the offices of Sarajevo's daily paper, *Oslobodjenje,* which consistently spoke out against the ethnic hatred some politicians sought to fuel in the former Yugoslavia. Shortly after the war began, Kemal Kurspahić, the paper's editor, told his staff, a Sarajevan mix of Serbs, Croats, and Bosnian Muslims, "All Sarajevo is under fire. We are in one of the most dangerous zones . . . Those who want to leave, can leave. And for those who want to keep working—we have to finish today's paper." Nobody left. *Oslobodjenje* was published that day—and every day for the next three years, throughout the deadly war.

Because few citizens had access to television or radio, and because the city was without electricity for much of the time and batteries were hard to come by, *Oslobodjenje* was almost the only reliable way of finding out the news. But, even as the demand for *Oslobodjenje* grew to levels greater than ever before, a paper shortage in the besieged city meant that the print run dropped to just a few thousand a day. People fought over the precious copies of the paper, eager to read a paper devoted to spreading the truth.

In a city where everything was in short supply, entrepreneurial Bosnians ensured that the maximum number of people could read the paper. In central Sarajevo, a pinned-up notice announced: "*Oslobodjenje* for rent. Price: one cigarette." People stood in line, giving up one of their much-needed smokes for the luxury of being able to read.

In June 1992, just a few months into the war, the Serb forces surrounding Sarajevo had fired incendiary shells at *Oslobodjenje*'s offices, and set the huge, tinted-glass tower ablaze, turning it into a blackened wreck. Still, though, the journalists continued working. The journalists moved into an underground bunker built originally to protect against nuclear attack, and worked seven-day shifts, to reduce the risk of being killed on the way to or from work. Freedom of expression, Kurspahić insisted, "cannot be silenced by cannons and tanks." One of the authors of this book visited the offices of *Oslobodjenje* at that time, and wrote then: "There are many minor miracles in Sarajevo. But *Oslobodjenje* is among the most remarkable." Those words still seem true today.

Cultural life continued in Sarajevo, too. Day after day, cellist Vedran Smajlović played Albinoni's "Adagio" on the site where a Serb mortar attack killed twenty-two people standing in line to buy bread on May 27, 1992.

The antiwar musical *Hair* was staged even as the killing worsened. In 1993, there was even an entire theater festival, with productions including a version of Samuel Beckett's *Waiting for Godot* directed by American author and activist Susan Sontag. The theme of *Godot,* in which the characters wait for a savior who is always expected but never appears (a young boy appears at one point to tell the two main characters, "Mr. Godot told me to tell you he won't come this evening, but surely tomorrow") was especially resonant in a city that felt so abandoned by the world. In the words of Sontag's Bosnian producer, Haris Pasović, "Every single day, we thought that our Godot would come, and every night we understood that he wouldn't."

From the comfort of their armchairs, some in the West criticized Sontag for her "war tourism." Bosnians saw it differently. They saw Sontag's theatrical project amid the gunfire as a reassurance that at least some people in the outside world cared. Sontag was made an honorary citizen of Sarajevo. In 2009, five years after her death and fourteen years after the end of the war, a square in Sarajevo was named after her.

Bosnians emphasized the importance of small things, too. Visitors frequently commented that the women of Sarajevo always seemed immaculately turned out, even when the barest necessities of life were often unavailable. The carefully applied lipstick and eyeliner represented, as Gordana Knežević, a journalist at *Oslobodjenje,* remarked at that time, "a civilized scorn for terror." In May 1993, Bosnians even organized a beauty contest, with an unusual banner unfurled on stage: "Don't Let Them Kill Us!"

The U2 song, "Miss Sarajevo," written as a sound track for Bill Carter's documentary of the same name, addresses the simple truth that Sarajevans yearned for nothing more than ordinariness:

> Is there a time for kohl and lipstick
> Is there a time for cutting hair
> Is there a time for high street shopping
> To find the right dress to wear

The answer, of course, was that there is no right or wrong time. Life must go on, even in the worst circumstances.

Sarajevo, Bosnia, 1993. They defied sniper's bullets and mortar shells to take part in a beauty contest.

Credit: Chris Helgren/Reuters

Producing a newspaper despite the snipers and the mortars; performing (and going to watch) *Hair* and *Godot;* applying lipstick and choosing the right dress to wear—each was an act of resistance all its own.

Shooting Star

Afghan Star, the equivalent of the *Pop Idol* and *American Idol* television talent contests, became massively popular in Afghanistan in recent years. Eleven million viewers—a third of the entire country—watched the 2007 finale. Millions texted in their votes by cell phone.

But participation in *Afghan Star* has meant much higher stakes in Afghanistan than *Idol* contests elsewhere. It became a reassertion of the right to make one's own choices in life. The television show proved to be a place where warlords wield no power and where millions of votes are cast in a contest that ordinary Afghans feel confident is free and fair.

Participants risked their lives by taking part in the show. The still-powerful Taliban argued that music is un-Islamic. Through their loyalty to *Afghan Star*, ordinary Afghans—particularly but not only the 60 percent of the population under twenty-one—showed that they disagreed. Havana Marking, director of an award-winning documentary about the *Afghan Star* contest, argued, "By creating something so popular, *Afghan Star* became a kind of identity or movement for the young people themselves. This is why the old guard is so frightened of it."

In her final song on stage, Setara Hussainzada, a twenty-two-year-old from Herat in western Afghanistan, broke a strict taboo by dancing before the cameras. As if public dancing by a woman weren't already defiance enough, her action became more extraordinary still when Hussainzada's headscarf slipped off and still she danced on regardless.

Ministers and warlords alike condemned her. Hussainzada received death threats. But she did not back down. After the program was over, she went on to become a professional singer in the Afghan capital, Kabul. Millions of Afghans continue enthusiastically to watch *Afghan Star*.

10

Bearing Witness

In a room where people unanimously maintain a conspiracy
of silence, one word of truth sounds like a pistol shot.

—Czesław Miłosz

The Emperor's Clothes

*The vilest scramble for loot that ever disfigured the history
of human conscience.*

—JOSEPH CONRAD

In the late nineteenth century, King Leopold II of Belgium
ruled the vast Congo—a single country similar in size to all
of western Europe—as his personal fiefdom. Ivory and rubber
from Congolese forests provided Leopold with huge profits.
In return, Congolese were abused, beaten, and killed. Millions
died. Despite the brutality, journalists and politicians alike
praised Leopold to the skies as an "example of humanity"
and a philanthropic monarch. The doggedness of Edmund
Dene Morel, junior clerk at a Liverpool-based shipping line,
changed that forever.

Elder Dempster, the company for which Morel worked,
enjoyed an exclusive contract with Leopold for shipping
goods to and from Congo. But on his trips to Antwerp, Morel
quickly noticed that something was seriously wrong.

Despite the huge value of the rubber and ivory shipped
out of Congo, the ships traveling to Congo carried little that
might be of value to the Congolese in return. There were
plenty of guns and bullets, but little else. Morel—who later
became friendly with Sir Arthur Conan Doyle, creator of
Sherlock Holmes—reached an inescapable conclusion. As
Morel himself wrote (quoted in Adam Hochschild's powerful
account, *King Leopold's Ghost*): "Forced labour of a terrible and
continuous kind could alone explain such unheard-of profits
. . . I was giddy and appalled at the cumulative significance
of my discoveries. It must be bad enough to stumble upon a

murder. I had stumbled upon a secret society of murderers with a King for a croniman."

Morel's employers wanted him to keep quiet. They did not want to lose the profitable Belgian contract. Morel refused. In 1901, at age twenty-eight, he resigned from Elder Dempster, determined to expose "a legalized infamy . . . accompanied by unimaginable barbarities responsible for vast destruction of human life."

Leopold's spokesmen repeatedly denied Morel's revelations. In response, Morel provided yet more incriminating documents (leaked by sympathetic insiders, who believed in the importance of his investigations). His mountains of documents proved beyond all doubt the cruelty that underlay the profits.

Leopold's agents tried to neutralize the impact of Morel's revelations—sometimes with threats, sometimes with attractive offers. On one occasion, Morel was invited to a dinner where, as he put it, "choice and copious wines" were served, accompanied by a lucrative hush-money proposal for dessert.

Morel refused the inducements.

In 1904, Morel met with Mark Twain, who penned *King Leopold's Soliloquy,* a satirical pamphlet in which Leopold rages at those like Morel who dare tell the truth about his brutal rule. Twain's Leopold complains that the newfangled camera is infuriatingly incorruptible: "Ten thousand pulpits and ten thousand presses are saying the good word for me all the time and placidly and convincingly denying the mutilations. Then that trivial little kodak, that a child can carry in its pocket, gets up, uttering never a word, and knocks them dumb!"

Morel ensured that the true story of life and death in Belgian-ruled Congo was loudly told. Philosopher Bertrand Russell said of him, "No other man known to me has had the same heroic simplicity in pursuing and proclaiming political truth."

Morel died in 1924, at age fifty-one. His work has important lessons for today, when the country now known as the Democratic Republic of Congo has again in recent years been mired in conflict over the natural resources it is privileged and cursed to possess in such abundance.

Train Ride to Global Movement

On November 19, 1960, Peter Benenson, a British lawyer, was on his daily commute to work on the London underground. On the train, he read a short news story about two Portuguese students who had been sentenced to seven years in jail. Their crime was to have raised their glasses in a Lisbon café in a toast to liberty, in defiance of the then-ruling dictator António Salazar.

Benenson, deeply affected by what he read, considered going to the Portuguese embassy to protest. Instead, he went to the nearby church of St. Martin-in-the-Fields on Trafalgar Square to sit and think. He resolved that something must be done to call attention to the plight of those locked up merely for the crime of speaking out.

On May 28, 1961, Benenson published a front-page article in the *Observer* newspaper, headlined "The Forgotten Prisoners." The article launched a campaign to gather evidence and raise public awareness to help free those imprisoned for their beliefs—what he called "prisoners of conscience."

Benenson wrote, "Open your newspaper any day of the week and you will find a report from somewhere in the world of someone being imprisoned, tortured or executed because his opinions or religion are unacceptable to his government . . . The newspaper reader feels a sickening sense of impotence. Yet if these feelings of disgust all over the world could be united into common action, something effective could be done."

The call to action prompted a huge response. Thousands wrote to Benenson to offer their support. The article was reprinted in many countries. It gave birth to the human rights organization Amnesty International.

As Benenson put it later, "It was necessary to think of a larger group which would harness the enthusiasm of people all over the world who were anxious to see a wider respect for human rights." The simple principle was that if governments knew they were being watched, and if the stories of unjustly imprisoned men and women were known, it would influence the actions of those governments.

One skeptic described the initiative as "one of the larger lunacies of our time." But the skeptics were proved wrong. One of the group's first successes came with the case of Archbishop Josef Beran, imprisoned by the Communist authorities in Czechoslovakia for fourteen years. Beran gained his freedom eighteen months after his case was adopted by the campaign and credited his release to the letter-writing efforts of the members of Amnesty International. Countless other prisoners of conscience have been released in the years since then.

Benenson continued battling for human rights until his death in 2005 at the age of eighty-three. Today, Amnesty International has two million members worldwide.

Catalog of Abuse

Between 1964 and 1979, Brazil was under military rule. Freedom of expression was restricted. The regime tortured and killed its citizens. Even after the generals officially handed power to a civilian government, they remained in powerful positions behind the scenes. The climate of fear was strong. In this halfway house—no longer a military dictatorship, but not yet free—a most extraordinary book was prepared in conditions of the utmost secrecy.

Brasil: Nunca Mais ("Brazil: Never Again"), published in 1985, contained graphic descriptions of torture, as practiced by the Brazilian military in past years. Some of the worst torturers still held powerful positions. The book was doubly powerful because it was based not on evidence gathered by others, but on the military's own records.

It all began with three churchmen. Jaime Wright, a Presbyterian minister whose brother was tortured and murdered by the military, first came up with the idea in 1979. Cardinal Paulo Arns, Catholic archbishop of São Paulo, enthusiastically backed the proposal. He stored secret materials on church premises, and became the project's patron. Philip Potter, Dominican-born general secretary of the World Council of Churches in Geneva, raised funds on behalf of his Brazilian colleagues.

Potter used the kind of financial secrecy more commonly associated with Mafia-style money laundering than with a church-funded book on human rights abuses. Hundreds of thousands of dollars were hand-carried from Geneva to Brazil. Worried about leaks, Cardinal Arns did not consult with his fellow bishops about the project; he did not even inform the Vatican.

The idea behind the Brazilian book was absurdly ambitious and breathtakingly simple. Secret military courts had kept detailed records of all trials—including descriptions from defendants of the torture that they had suffered. Lawrence Weschler, author of *A Miracle, a Universe: Settling Accounts with Torturers,* quotes Wright: "The Brazilian generals . . . never imagined they'd be held accountable to anyone. But the forms, the technicalities, required complete and well-ordered records, so they kept them."

The authors of *Brasil: Nunca Mais* got their hands on the torture records by having trusted lawyers request individual files for their clients. (Access was available under a new amnesty law. The rule was that each file could be kept for twenty-four hours before it had to be returned.) The sometimes massive files were quickly duplicated on three photocopiers in an anonymous office suite the collaborators had rented in the capital, Brasilia. The next day, more files were checked out, and the process began all over again. The secretly assembled team copied from morning until night—day after day, seven days a week. From Brasilia, the material was taken to a place of greater safety—an anonymous, locked room belonging to the Catholic archdiocese in São Paulo. From there, in turn, microfilms were carried to Geneva. In all, a million pages were copied. Edited down, those testimonies formed the basis for the historically explosive book.

By design, *Brasil: Nunca Mais* had the opposite of a high-profile launch when it first slipped into Brazilian bookshops on July 15, 1985. Cardinal Arns insisted in advance that the publishers would only be permitted to publish *Brasil: Nunca Mais* if they guaranteed that there would be no advance publicity, and no announcement of the release date. In order to ensure the book's security, this was in every respect an "under-the-radar" release. And yet, within just a few weeks, *Brasil: Nunca Mais* rose to number one on the national best-seller lists.

The military launched a massive (and fruitless) investigation into how the book had been published. The Supreme Military Court even met to discuss using still-existing security laws to ban the book altogether. That never happened: The generals realized, perhaps, that efforts to suppress *Brasil: Nunca Mais* would only backfire—not least since an English translation had in the meantime appeared in the United States, which would make a Brazilian ban largely futile.

The book remained in the Brazilian best-seller lists for two years. It became the best-selling work of nonfiction in the country's history. On September 23, 1985, just two months after the publication of *Brasil: Nunca Mais,* Brazil signed the United Nations convention against torture.

Truth from the Grave

In June 2009, on the twentieth anniversary of the Tiananmen Square massacre in Beijing, the Chinese authorities were eager to bury any discussion of what China officially describes as the Tiananmen "incident." Untold numbers—hundreds, perhaps thousands—of peaceful protesters died on June 4, 1989. And yet, the word *massacre* is banned. The courage of one man helped ensure that the truth about Tiananmen Square can never be entirely suppressed.

Zhao Ziyang was deposed as Chinese Communist Party leader in 1989 because he spoke out against the killings of students at Tiananmen Square. In the years before his death in 2005, at age eighty-five, Zhao worked secretly to ensure that the official, whitewashed version of history would not survive. For years after 1989, Zhao was kept under house arrest. (On a few occasions, to his captors' irritation, he slipped out to play golf.) Under his guards' noses, however, he secretly recorded dozens of cassette tapes—thirty hours' worth in all—exposing the truth about how and why the Tiananmen massacre happened.

The Chinese authorities would have gone to any lengths to suppress Zhao's journal, if they had learned of its existence. They never guessed. Zhao gave tapes to a few trusted friends, for publication after his death. The complete collection of original cassettes was hidden in plain sight—in Zhao's study, among his grandchildren's toys.

The memoirs contained revelations about the decision to launch a lethal crackdown, and were deeply damaging to the Chinese authorities when the book was published on the occasion of the twentieth anniversary of the massacre. The government wants people not to think about the events of Tiananmen Square at all. The publication of Zhao's memoir in 2009 made that impossible. In Hong Kong, booksellers said that *Prisoner of the State: The Secret Journal of Premier Zhao Ziyang* was the most sought-after book in twenty years. In mainland China, where Zhao's name has been airbrushed from history, the authorities tried hard to suppress the book. Despite that, it quickly became an online hit.

Zhao's act of defiance, coming even as it did from beyond the grave, forced a confrontation with historical truth—the truth that the Chinese authorities fear most. As *Time* magazine had already noted at the time of Zhao's death in 2005, Zhao "may be more dangerous in death than he was in life."

A Tidy Case

In the 1980s, Hissène Habré was the repressive, U.S.-backed leader of Chad in central Africa. He was responsible for tens of thousands of deaths during his eight years in power, and yet remained untouchable—immune to retribution for his tyranny. Even after Habré's fall in 1990, most Chadians assumed he would never be held responsible for the crimes committed during his years in power. If that looks different today, it has much to do with the determination of two men: Souleymane Guengueng, a Chadian accountant and human rights activist (who had himself been incarcerated in Habré's prisons), and Reed Brody, a lawyer with Human Rights Watch nicknamed the "dictator-hunter."

Guengueng and his colleagues were determined to see that Habré's crimes were recorded and those responsible for them punished. They interviewed hundreds of torture victims and collated the damning evidence. Guengueng hid files in a trunk at his home. Brody found additional incriminating documents in the chaos of Habré's abandoned secret police headquarters. For years, it seemed impossible that any of this could have consequences. But, not least because of Brody's and Guengueng's work, things are changing.

In 2007, the West African state of Senegal, where Habré had found exile, authorized its courts to prosecute the former dictator. In Belgium, Habré has been indicted for crimes against humanity. As Brody pointed out in Klaartje Quirijns's documentary, *The Dictator Hunter,* "If you kill one person, you go to jail. If you kill forty people, they put you in an insane asylum. But if you kill forty thousand people, you get a comfortable exile with a bank account in another country."

That is what Guengueng and Brody have sought to change. Without the determination of these two men, there would be no chance that Habré might face justice. Because of Guengueng and Brody, however, the clock is ticking. In Guengueng's words, "I will not feel complete until Habré is in jail. We are doing this to prevent it from happening again, for future generations."

11

Marshalling Arts

Like cannons hidden in flowers.
—Robert Schumann on the subversive impact of Chopin's piano music.
(Schumann suggested that the Russian tsar would ban the
Polish composer's music, if only he understood its power.)

Rocking Revolution

True, the Plastic People of the Universe, who liked to perform in hippie-ish robes, might not have seemed like the most obvious people to threaten a government that came to power on the back of tanks. But that was not how Czechoslovakia's loyal pro-Moscow Communists saw the band in the years following the Russian invasion of 1968.

The Plastic People were fans of Andy Warhol and the music of the Velvet Underground. Their lyrics seemed distinctly apolitical: "We will sleep all day, we will hide our pale bodies under the crimson feathers. Our long black hair we will wrap around our heads . . ." one typical song declared.

Not very subversive stuff, most might agree. But the Plastic People dared to be different. That was in itself a dangerous challenge to the regime. Concerts by the Plastic People were prohibited.

The band quickly found ways to get around the ban. A concert might masquerade as an art history lecture, which meant a brief discussion of Andy Warhol, which would lead to discussion of the Velvet Underground, which in turn provided the excuse for a few hours of Plastic People music. On other occasions, concerts were disguised as private parties. One divorced couple even got remarried, just to provide the Plastics with an excuse to play.

Police beat and arrested their fans—most famously at what became known as the "České Budějovice massacre." On March 29, 1974, a thousand fans showed up in the town of České Budějovice to hear the Plastics perform. Hundreds of fans were beaten with clubs, herded onto a waiting train, and sent back to Prague. The Plastics did not perform that night—but they continued to organize their illegal concerts, which continued to enrage the regime.

Finally, the authorities decided that this determination to play music that had not been officially sanctioned needed to be stopped, once and for all. On March 17, 1976, in response to a music festival in the town of Bojanovice, twenty-seven people, including the Plastic People, were arrested and charged with "organized disturbance of the peace." Their songs were said to have "an antisocial impact, extolling nihilism, decadence, and clericalism." (In other words: The musicians didn't seem to take the government seriously enough.)

The jail sentences proved, however, to be the beginning—not the end—of the difficulties for the regime.

Partly as a result of the arrest of this apolitical rock band—whose story is partly retold in Tom Stoppard's 2006 play *Rock 'n' Roll*—playwright Václav Havel and other dissidents came together to publish the landmark dissident document Charter 77. Charter 77, which was published on New Year's Day 1977, demanded freedom of expression and a range of other basic rights. The protest document specifically referred in that context to "the trials of young musicians now going on"—in other words, the jailed Plastic People of the Universe. As Havel himself later noted, he and the other signatories came together "in defence of those unknown musicians . . . and became 'well-known dissidents' precisely because of that."

The velvet revolution of November 1989—when the Communist regime ended without a shot being fired—can be seen as the culmination of the changes the Plastics helped unleash thirteen years earlier.

Police violence against a student-led protest in Prague on November 17, 1989 triggered much larger demonstrations in the days to come, including by older Czechs who had until then been hesitant but became defiant because of the violence. Hundreds of thousands of protesters filled Wenceslas Square in the center of the Czech capital, defying the police to beat them, too. The square was filled with the sounds of tinkling bells and jangling keys, echoing the traditional words at the end of Czech children's stories: "The bell is ringing—and the story is over."

As the crowds continued to grow, pressure increased for the unelected rulers to pack their bags and go. Astonishingly, they did. The hard-line leadership resigned after just a week's worth of mass jangled keys. Plastics fan Václav Havel—whom Communist prime minister Ladislav Adamec had publicly described as "a nobody" just a few months earlier—became his country's leader.

On the twentieth anniversary of Charter 77 in 1997, the protester-turned-president invited the band to play a reunion concert in the presidential palace. Band member Milan Hlavsa explained that the Plastic People did not start off with the intention of destroying Communism. "But if we helped," he said, "we are glad."

The Plastic People were not the only Czech musicians who became synonymous with change. On November 24, 1989—the historic culminating day of Czechoslovakia's velvet revolution—Václav Havel and Alexander Dubček, the reformist leader ousted by Russian tanks in 1968, both spoke. It was a politically momentous occasion. But for many Czechs who were in the square that day, the music performed was equally memorable.

Marta Kubišová, the country's most adored singer, had been banned for twenty years after the Soviet invasion. Her song, "Prayer for Marta," had been a kind of unofficial hymn of resistance to the tanks. When she stepped onto the balcony overlooking Wenceslas Square and began to sing the long-banned "Prayer for Marta," the crowds cheered and wept.

A few hours later, the Communist leadership resigned. Kubišová's iconic voice ("Let them pass! Let them pass already!") had helped send them on their way.

Choirs against Tanks

In June 1940, as part of the secret terms of the Molotov-Ribbentrop pact agreed between Hitler and Stalin the previous year, the Soviet Union occupied the independent Baltic state of Estonia, along with its neighbors Latvia and Lithuania. The Soviet regime tried to snuff out all memory of Estonia's national identity. For almost half a century, flying the Estonian blue, black, and white national flag (blue for the sky, black for the soil, white for the aspirations of the Estonian people) became a crime punishable by imprisonment or by being sent to a Siberian labor camp.

In spring 1988, Estonians found a discreet way of striking back. For public protests, Estonians started buying three separate banners—one blue, one white, one black. When flown together, the three colors became the illegal flag. When separated, they were innocent pieces of material once more.

That small defiance was just a prologue for what was yet to come. Another crucial weapon in the bloodless revolution against the Russian tanks proved to be old folk songs.

Estonians had always been proud of their song festival. Since 1869, massed choirs gathered every few years to sing national songs. During half a century of Soviet occupation, many songs were forbidden. In the summer of 1988, however, the crowds found their voices.

A pop concert on June 11, 1988 in the Estonian capital, Tallinn, became a defiant performance of long-banned songs. Thousands marched to the song festival grounds on the edge of the town, and the concert continued into the night. Night after night for the next week, more and more came to take part—singing songs that celebrated Estonia's lost independence and expressing wonder at what they had themselves unleashed. By the end of the week, the crowds reached 100,000.

Songs with titles like "Cherishing the Beauty of the Land of My Fathers" might not sound revolutionary. But they implied a memory of Estonian independence, and thus challenged the very foundations of Soviet power. As one participant interviewed for James and Maureen Tusty's 2008 documentary *The Singing Revolution* remembered: "Singing together—that was our power."

Then, on September 11, 1988, 300,000 Estonians—a third of the country's population—gathered at the festival grounds for the Song of Estonia, a concert and political rally combined. More banned music was sung, more banned flags were waved. The momentum of change had dramatically grown during the three months since the concerts in June. In a phrase that quickly caught on, artist

Heinz Valk told the crowds, "One day, no matter what, we will win!"

In what soon became known as Estonia's singing revolution, those weeks transformed the country. Two months later, in November 1988, the Estonian parliament—to the fury of Soviet leader Mikhail Gorbachev and his Communist comrades—declared sovereignty from Moscow. It was just the first of a series of acts of defiance. From then on, there would be no turning back. As an Estonian activist told one of the authors of this book in August 1989, at the time of the fiftieth anniversary of the Hitler-Stalin pact (whose secret terms Moscow still refused to admit): "You can't put toothpaste back in the tube . . .We will win eventually, sooner or later."

He was right. Violent attempts by Moscow to end all the changes in the Baltic states—in January 1991, and again in August of that year—both ended badly for the men with tanks. International recognition of Estonia followed soon after the collapse of the Soviet coup in August 1991. By the end of 1991, the Soviet colossus itself was history. The singing of a few folk songs helped trigger the collapse of the seventy-four-year-old Soviet empire.

Radio Days

When Serb leader Slobodan Milošević came to power in 1989, he clamped down harshly on the media. Through Milošević's warmongering decade in power, Radio B92, a popular news and music station in the Serb capital, Belgrade, was repeatedly closed down because it dared to maintain a steadfastly independent voice.

On one occasion, during violently dispersed demonstrations in 1991, the authorities forbade B92 to broadcast news, except as provided by the government news agency. Only music was permitted. B92 complied, after a fashion. It broadcast a nonstop diet of music that reflected the officially sponsored violence on the streets outside—songs like The Clash's "White Riot," and Thin Lizzy's "The Boys Are Back in Town." One song was repeated over and over—Public Enemy's "Fight the Power." "The regime didn't understand music," Veran Matić, director of B92, later told Matthew Collin, author of *This is Serbia Calling: Rock 'n' Roll Radio and Belgrade's Underground Resistance*. "But the listeners could understand the code."

Even as the state descended into political madness through the 1990s, loyal progovernment radio stations provided an accompanying sound track of what became known as "turbofolk," whose upbeat rhythms and nationalist lyrics the regime deemed to be good for citizens' souls. As Serb journalist Teofil Pančić later remembered, "On state radio, you had so-called folk singers singing songs about Greater Serbia and how we all love our motherland and how we should all be willing to kill and be killed for it . . . What B92 and others did was celebrate life. That's the difference."

At one point, the government took B92 over completely, evicting the station's own staff. The authorities seemed to believe that if the news bulletins were turned into progovernment propaganda—"President Milošević receives a delegation from the Communist Party of China" was one exciting headline, broadcast by the puppet B92—that would be a victory. But the real B92 got back on the air via the then-still-new Internet. Neither the music nor the news bulletins were entirely silenced.

October 5, 2000 was the final day of Serbia's peaceful revolution in response to an election that Milošević had tried to steal (photoshopped crowds and confiscated empty boxes, as described in Chapter 5, did not help the Serb leader survive). One of the authors of this book joined the massive traffic jams that clogged all the roads leading into Belgrade as hundreds of thousands of Serbs descended on the capital to make it clear to Milošević that it really was time to go. The traffic jams included a yellow bulldozer, whose owner drove it across the country and then up the parliament steps. (Some have called this the bulldozer revolution.)

As the regime collapsed at the end of that extraordinary day, B92 reoccupied its own studios. The unwanted occupiers had fled in haste. When Sasha Mirković of B92 walked back into his office, he found condoms and an unfinished cup of coffee on the desk. In Mirković's words: "It felt like someone had been wearing my underpants. We're going to need some powerful disinfectant in here."

Radio B92 remains an independent voice in Belgrade. The station's playlist can afford to be less political these days.

Command Performance

The play's the thing
Wherein I'll catch the conscience of the king.
—WILLIAM SHAKESPEARE, *Hamlet*

Robert Mugabe, who came to power in Zimbabwe as a liberation hero in 1979, ruled with increasing brutality over the years. Opposition leaders and human rights activists were arrested, tortured, and killed. Under Mugabe's corrupt rule, the once-flourishing economy was destroyed; inflation reached an unimaginable 500 quintillion percent. Even while criticism was forbidden, some found ways to confront the president publicly—by making people laugh.

Just a few months before historic elections in 2008—which, despite all the violence against opposition supporters, sought to challenge Mugabe as never before— actors Anthony Tongani and Silvanos Mudzvova staged a comedy called *The Final Push.*

The Final Push was about a Mugabe-like chairman of a building called Liberty House and his challenger, a version of opposition leader Morgan Tsvangirai. The two men get stuck in an elevator during a power outage. At one point, they slug it out in a boxing match.

The audience loved the disrespectful play. Unsurprisingly, the police did not. Tongani and Mudzvova were both arrested.

So far, so normal in a police state. But things did not end there. The two men were ordered to re-perform their play at the police station, so that the authorities could check just how unacceptable the play was.

Then they were told to perform it again.

And again.

And . . . twelve times altogether, over the span of two days.

Embarrassingly, some of the uniformed policemen admitted to finding the performance entertaining. They laughed in the right places (including when the chairman of Liberty House gets knocked out). The representatives of the CIO, Mugabe's secret police, did not find it funny.

Mudzvova and Tongani were first charged with inciting the masses to revolt, then with breach of the censorship law. Mudzvova remained defiant, telling Robyn Dixon of the *Los Angeles Times:* "Artists, like everybody else, fear for their lives. But the moment you have that fear, you won't get anywhere." The offending knockout scene was dropped from *The Final Push* to placate the authorities (and then promptly reinstated).

When Mugabe lost the 2008 elections, he refused to acknowledge the election's outcome and decided to remain in power. Only a year later did he finally give way to some of the pressures, by allowing Tsvangirai, whose fictional alter ego defeated Mugabe in the elevator, to become prime minister as part of what was described as a power-sharing arrangement. In reality, President Mugabe continues at the time of this writing to hold all the real power. He refuses to reform the security forces, and violence against opposition supporters has continued.

Mudzvova and his colleagues, meanwhile, continue to make Zimbabwean audiences laugh, even as they confront the failures of the country's lawless president.

An Irrepressible Voice

Marian Anderson was America's best-known singer, an acknowledged international star. In the 1930s, she sang in prestigious concert halls all across Europe. In Salzburg, the acclaimed conductor Arturo Toscanini came to her dressing room and told her, "Yours is a voice such as one hears once in a hundred years."

Her popularity and her artistic talent were, however, not enough for some—as Anderson's manager, Sol Hurok, discovered when he tried to book Anderson at Washington's largest venue, Constitution Hall, in 1939.

Built just eleven years earlier, Constitution Hall was established and managed by the Daughters of the American Revolution, an organization of descendants of those who fought for and won American independence. When Hurok tried to arrange a booking for Anderson for Easter 1939, he was told that the hall was already booked.

It soon became clear that that was a lie. Further inquiries revealed that the hall remained ready to offer Easter dates to other artists—for example, the pianist Ignacy Jan Paderewski. But not for Anderson. When challenged, the hall's manager spelled things out more bluntly, as described in Raymond Arsenault's *The Sound of Freedom*. "No date," the manager shouted, "will *ever* be available for Marian Anderson in Constitution Hall!"

The problem was simple: Anderson was black.

News of the decision sparked public outcry. Jascha Heifetz, perhaps the world's most famous violinist, said: "It made me feel ashamed. I protest, as the entire musical profession protests, against such a sad and deplorable attitude." The Daughters of the Revolution, however, refused to back down. They voted 39 to 1 to keep the color ban. In response, one of the most famous Daughters, First Lady Eleanor Roosevelt, resigned in protest.

Anderson had been denied an important stage, but she was about to grace a much greater one. If Anderson could not sing inside Washington's largest venue, seating four thousand, what about singing at the Lincoln Memorial, where space was unlimited? President Roosevelt, not least with the help of his wife, was easily persuaded. He told Harold Ickes, secretary of the interior: "She can sing from the top of the Washington monument if she wants to."

The popular response was unprecedented. On Easter Sunday, 1939, a crowd of 75,000, black and white, gathered to hear her sing. Millions more waited by their radios for the live broadcast. Anderson opened with "My Country, 'Tis of Thee," including the third verse which resonantly declares:

> Let music swell the breeze,
> And ring from all the trees
> Sweet freedom's song;
> Let mortal tongues awake;
> Let all that breathe partake;
> Let rocks their silence break,
> The sound prolong.

The sound was indeed prolonged. Four years after the Lincoln Memorial concert, the Daughters of the American Revolution relented and invited Marian Anderson to sing to a multiracial audience at Constitution Hall.

A quarter of a century after Anderson's historic performance, Martin Luther King Jr. told a crowd of a quarter of a million people gathered at the Lincoln Memorial, on August 28, 1963: "I have a dream." Anderson was present for King's speech and sang again on that day. Forty-six years later, at the same memorial in 2009, Aretha Franklin sang "My Country, 'Tis of Thee," to mark the occasion when a newly inaugurated African-American president of the United States would address the world.

Freedom Song

With this film and this music, I feel closer to God than before
—Bahman Ghobadi, director of the 2009 Iranian film
Nobody Knows About Persian Cats, banned for its vivid
depiction of the forbidden music scene in Tehran

She is the most celebrated recording artist in Iranian history. Her status has been compared to that of Elvis, Marilyn Monroe, and the Beatles rolled into one. When the acclaimed singer Googoosh walked onto the stage of the Pacific Coliseum sports stadium in Vancouver on August 8, 2000, it was her first public performance in more than twenty years. Before singing the first note, she told the huge crowd, "I wish all Iranians could be here with me tonight."

It was the sentiment of an artist denied the right to perform for her adoring fans in her own country. After the revolution in 1979, the new Islamic Republic of Iran had banned women from singing in public, believing that their voices would corrupt men. Googoosh's career was frozen at the age of twenty-eight. The government forbade her to perform at home and denied her a passport for the next two decades—even while her popularity among Iranians remained undiminished. Of her concert in Canada in 2000, she said, "My singing on the stage again is a sort of hope in itself."

The next Googoosh may be waiting in the wings. Despite all the prohibitions against public singing, women in Iran have found ways to express themselves through music. One woman—who wanted to make music, no matter what the cost—may yet have an impact on political change, from beyond the grave.

On June 20, 2009, twenty-six-year-old Neda Agha-Soltan was shot and killed at an antigovernment protest in Iran, where hundreds of thousands protested against what they saw as election theft by President Mahmoud Ahmadinejad. In a shocking few seconds of video, seen in Iran and around the world, Neda bled to death as those around her pleaded, "Don't go!"

Neda—who earlier that day told her anxious mother, "If I don't go out, who will?"—was accompanied by her music teacher at the time of her death. Despite the ban on women performers, she had been taking singing lessons, and loved to sing the songs of Googoosh. Neda means "the voice" in Persian, and that was how she became known to millions.

Neda and her voice became a symbol of Iranian defiance. On the fortieth day after her death, a traditional day of mourning, thousands defied beatings and tear gas to gather in her memory. (A secretly filmed documentary, *For Neda*, was released a year after her death. The authorities tried to block broadcasts of the film, which can be seen on YouTube; *For Neda* quickly went viral on the Internet and was watched by millions in Iran.)

In response to Neda's death, Iran's eighty-two-year-old national poet, Simin Behbahani, wrote (translated by Iran Davar Ardalan):

> You are neither dead, nor will you die.
> You will always remain alive.
> You have an eternal existence.
> You are the voice of the people of Iran.

The massive protests on the streets of Tehran, and the deaths of Neda and other protesters, prompted Googoosh to make her first foray into politics. At a rally at the United Nations in New York in July 2009, she said that her hope for Iran was "freedom of expression, freedom of the pen, freedom of thought, freedom of elections, freedom of religion, and freedom for women."

Her conclusion: "We will not tremble, we will not fall, we will not lose."

12

Just Law

Legislation won't change the heart,
but it will restrain the heartless.
                                                    —Martin Luther King Jr.

Seriously Hoaxed

Multinational chemical companies are frequently unembarrassable. But two men succeeded in dramatically embarrassing the huge Dow Chemical Company, with one of the most astonishing hoaxes in history. They hope the impact of that hoax may yet help contribute to a historic change of heart.

On December 3, 1984, forty tons of deadly gas leaked from a pesticide factory in Bhopal, India, which belonged to the U.S.-owned Union Carbide, in what is widely acknowledged as the worst industrial disaster in the world. In *Clouds of Injustice,* a report published on the twentieth anniversary in 2004, Amnesty International estimated that 7,000 died in the first few days after the explosion, and a further 15,000 in subsequent years. The report noted: "The plant site has still not been cleaned up so toxic wastes continue to pollute the environment and contaminate water that surrounding communities rely on. And, astonishingly, no one has been held to account for the leak and its appalling consequences." Indra Sinha, author of *Animal's People,* which tells the story of the disaster, described the aftermath:

> The sun came up on choking, blinded people making their way to the hospitals. Some, desperate to relieve the agony in their eyes, were washing them in sewage water from the open drains.

> The hospitals were full of the dying and doctors did not know how to treat them because they did not know which gas or gases had leaked, and Union Carbide would not release the information, claiming it was a "trade secret."

In 2001, Dow Chemical bought Union Carbide. Dow insists that all liabilities have been settled. In India, the catastrophe has remained a live issue for a quarter of a century. In the United States, where Dow Chemical has its headquarters, the accident has been mostly forgotten.

Two men, armed with nothing but a social conscience and a bright idea, sought to change that.

In advance of the twentieth anniversary of the Bhopal accident in 2004, Andy Bichlbaum and Mike Bonanno—New York-based social activists who describe themselves as the Yes Men—set up a website, dowethics.com, which purported to represent Dow Chemical. The website triggered a request from BBC World Television for a Dow representative to give an interview on the occasion of the anniversary. Bichlbaum duly transformed himself into the besuited "Jude Finisterra," a fictional spokesman for Dow.

Speaking live to a startled BBC interviewer and to millions of viewers worldwide, Bichlbaum agreed that Dow took full responsibility for the disaster for the first time. Then Bichlbaum announced a $12 billion plan to compensate victims and organize a full cleanup. (The preparations for the interview, and the interview itself, can be seen in Bichlbaum's and Bonanno's 2009 documentary film, *The Yes Men Fix the World*.)

The dramatic news of Dow's expensive change of heart bounced around the world, causing a loss of $2 billion in the company's value within just a few hours. When the stunt was exposed (and the value of Dow shares bounced back up again), "Finisterra" was invited back on television the same evening to explain the Yes Men's action. This time, he appeared as Bichlbaum.

Some accused the Yes Men of bringing false hope to the people of Bhopal. But the Yes Men's BBC stunt helped shine a spotlight on the forgotten suffering caused by the deadly accident. When Bichlbaum and Bonanno later visited Bhopal, local activists gave them a warm welcome. The two men were praised for their impudent hoax, which ensured that the suffering of the people of Bhopal became a focus of worldwide attention, despite those who wanted the subject to be buried. In the Yes Men's own words, "Sometimes it takes a lie to expose the truth."

Drawing a Line

Treat them with humanity, and let them have no reason to complain of us copying the brutal manner of the British army . . . While we are contending for our own liberty we should be very cautious of violating the rights of conscience in others.

—George Washington, giving instructions
in 1777 on how to treat British prisoners

Alberto Mora was U.S. general naval counsel with a rank equivalent to that of a four-star general when he learned in 2002 that the U.S. administration was opening the door to torture. "Unlawful enemy combatants," held by U.S. forces at Guantánamo Bay, were placed on a leash, interrogated for twenty hours at a time, or deprived of sleep for days. Standing up to his country's leaders, Mora opposed the idea that it was moral, legal, or useful to carry out torture, at a time when too few were ready to do so.

Mora knew about terrorism firsthand. He had been inside the Pentagon when one of the 9/11 planes crashed into the building. But he did not believe that the threat of terrorism meant basic rules of humanity could be abandoned. "The debate here isn't only how to protect the country," he later told Jane Mayer of the *New Yorker*. "It's how to protect our values."

A now notorious, then still-secret memo from President George W. Bush's Justice Department, written in August 2002, sought to define torture almost out of existence. Mora, whose seniority allowed him to see the memo, criticized what he described as the "catastrophically poor legal reasoning." In February 2003—a year before the Abu Ghraib scandal broke—Mora invited John Yoo, chief author of the memo, to discuss the conclusions.

"Are you saying the president has the authority to order torture?" a disbelieving Mora asked. "Yes," Yoo replied.

Mora wanted the Yoo memo to be locked away and "never let out to see the light of day." Instead, those White House-approved conclusions were put into practice at the U.S.-administered Bagram Air Base in Afghanistan, at Guantánamo, and at Abu Ghraib in Iraq.

Mora was not alone in arguing that breaking the rules does nothing to keep the world safe. A number of military lawyers insisted, despite all the pressures from their political bosses, that justice must be done and seen to be done.

Lieutenant-Commander Charles Swift, for example, challenged the lawlessness of the indefinite detention at Guantánamo all the way up to the Supreme Court on behalf of Salim Hamdan, a Yemeni who served as Osama bin Laden's driver. As the *New York Times* later noted, Hamdan's offenses were not enumerated anywhere, "but appear to include checking the oil and the tire pressure." The U.S. Supreme Court ruling on June 29, 2006 for Swift and his client in the case of *Rumsfeld v. Hamdan* was a blow for President Bush's policies. The judgment was, the *New York Times* wrote, "an important and welcome reaffirmation that even in times of war, the law is what the Constitution, the statute books and the Geneva Conventions say it is—not what the president wants it to be." Shortly after the Supreme Court decided in Swift's favor—and against the U.S. government—Swift was told that he must retire, allegedly because of promotion policies.

Lieutenant-Commander Matthew Diaz—who had been the subject of a glowing profile in the official Guantánamo newsletter, *Behind the Wire*—was another of those who stood up for the rule of law. Diaz had been shocked at the government's refusal to hand over the names of Guantánamo detainees, as that refusal made it impossible for the men to receive independent legal advice. And so he secretly copied hundreds of names and sent them to the Center for Constitutional Rights in New York, hidden inside a giant, cartoon-puppy Valentine's card, which he bought at the Guantánamo store. For that crime, Diaz was convicted of disclosing information that "could be used to the injury of the United States," and sentenced to six months in jail. He remains unrepentant, saying: "There was nothing else that I could really do."

Resisters like Mora, Swift, and Diaz were in a minority during America's bleak torture-permissive era, from 2002 to 2008. But their quiet defiance played an important role in making people understand and turn away from the evil of government-sanctioned torture.

"When you put together the pieces, it's all so sad," Mora says now. "To preserve flexibility, they were willing to throw away our values." Diaz quotes the words of Supreme Court Justice Louis Brandeis, writing in 1928: "If the government becomes a lawbreaker, it breeds contempt for the law and invites every man to become a law unto itself."

Fellow Americans

After the Japanese bombing of Pearl Harbor in 1942, around 120,000 people of Japanese descent in the United States were forced out of their homes and interned. Many approved of the policy, arguing that this was the only way to keep the country safe. The governor of Wyoming talked approvingly of "Japs hanging from every pine tree." The attorney general of Idaho said, "We want to keep this a white man's country." In a climate where Japanese-Americans were perceived as the enemy, one politician took a very different tack—and destroyed his own career by doing so.

Ralph Carr, governor of Colorado, was a political star, mentioned as a possible future president. All such prospects vanished when Carr spoke out against demonizing American Japanese. After insisting that "We cannot test the degree of a man's affection for his country by the birthplace of his grandfather," Carr was pilloried and threatened with impeachment, as described in Adam Schrager's biography of Carr, *The Principled Politician*. After running in 1942 for a Senate seat, Carr lost to the Democratic incumbent, in part because of his vocal objection to anti-Japanese sentiment. He withdrew from politics and died in 1950.

The internment of Japanese Americans was later acknowledged to have been based on fear and prejudice rather than any real evidence of a sabotage threat. Four decades later, in 1988, President Ronald Reagan signed legislation officially apologizing for the Japanese internment, calling it "a failure of political leadership."

In 1942, the *Denver Post* had insisted that "Colorado doesn't want these yellow devils." The paper's outspoken support of the internment policy helped push Carr toward oblivion. Fifty-seven years later, the *Post* changed its mind. It named Carr as Colorado's Person of the Century. "What he did was take a stand," the paper noted. "In one of America's darkest hours, he defended humanity and decency . . . [in] a move that cost him a career."

One for All

Helen Suzman grew up in a life of privilege in apartheid South Africa. But she loathed the injustice of a system that denied blacks even the most basic rights.

In 1953, she was elected as opposition United Party member of the South African parliament. Six years later, unhappy with the party's failure to confront apartheid directly, she cofounded the Progressive Party, which opposed all racial discrimination. In 1961, she was elected the Progressive Party's sole member of parliament, now separated from her former

United Party colleagues on the parliamentary benches. In that isolated context, surrounded by those who supported or condoned racist policies, it seemed she could change nothing. And yet, she relentlessly wore the government down.

In parliament, she highlighted the absurdity of the definitions clause in the Race Classifications Act, which created a bizarre South African color chart of identity—black, white, colored, Indian, each with different rights or lack of rights. She asked endless questions about how many blacks under the act had become colored and how many coloreds had been reclassified as white; how many whites had been reclassified as blacks, how many Indians had been reclassified . . . and so on. Her questions exposed the ludicrousness of the rules, and the human tragedy affecting every detail of people's lives: where they could live, where they could work, who they could and could not marry.

In 1960, events at Sharpeville, south of Johannesburg, changed history. On March 21, police opened fire on blacks peacefully protesting against the arbitrary cruelty of the pass laws, which divided families and determined who could live or work where. The shooting continued, even as crowds tried to flee. Sixty-nine people were killed.

The South African government declared a state of emergency. New laws made it possible to intern people without trial. Eighteen thousand people, including protesters and most of the country's leading anti-apartheid activists, were held without charge. Suzman was the only member of parliament to speak out against the official lawlessness, which, she said, brought South Africa "further into the morass of a totalitarian state."

When members of parliament voted on internment, the speaker of the House would say: "I put the question, those in favor say 'Aye' and those against say 'Nay.'" When only Suzman raised her voice in opposition, the speaker proclaimed: "The ayes have it."

Suzman used parliamentary procedures to emphasize the political shame. She used her right as a member of parliament to call for members to stand up and physically vote with their feet, by calling "Divide!" This obliged the supine opposition to cross the floor to join the ruling Nationalist Party members of parliament and thus make clear where they stood when they voted in favor of detention without trial. Suzman repeatedly entered the "no" lobby alone.

The system was eventually changed, requiring at least four members of parliament (instead of just one) to call "Divide!" rather than merely allowing members to shout "Aye!" or "Nay!" from their seats. Soon after, five Progressive Party members were elected, so Suzman was not yet silenced. The cries of "Divide!" and the walks of shame continued.

In other respects, too, Suzman was a lone parliamentary voice. Members of parliament were allowed to visit Robben Island, where Nelson Mandela and others were sentenced to life imprisonment in 1964. Suzman was, however, the only person who took advantage of the opportunity.

As Mandela later wrote in his memoirs, "Mrs. Suzman— all five feet two inches of her—came through the door of our passageway . . . It was an odd and wonderful sight to see this courageous woman peering into our cells and strolling around our courtyard. She was the first and only woman ever to grace our cells."

Suzman regularly received death threats. But even those who threatened her perhaps came to regret it. Her method of dealing with the late-night callers was always the same. She blew a shrill whistle into the phone, which she always kept handy. She would hear a groan at the other end. "I seldom heard the same voice," she noted.

Her only regret, she told the BBC later, was to have retired from politics in 1989, just one year before Mandela was released and the dismantling of apartheid began. In 1990, the laws she had fought against for so long began to be repealed. Mandela talked of her "fortitude that draws its strength from the conviction that no person can be free while others are unfree."

Suzman died on New Year's Day 2009, at age ninety-one. As she herself said, paraphrasing U.S. President Theodore Roosevelt: "I did what I could, where I was, with what I had."

Accounts and Accountability

Never doubt that a small group of thoughtful, committed citizens can change the world. Indeed, it is the only thing that ever has.

—MARGARET MEAD

Katie Redford, a twenty-five-year-old student at the University of Virginia School of Law, was doing a human rights internship on the Thai-Burmese border in 1993. During her time there, she heard many stories of villagers fleeing from military-ruled Burma into Thailand. The

Burmese army terrorized communities as entire villages were destroyed to clear a corridor for a gas pipeline being built for the California-based oil company, Unocal, and its partners, including the French oil company, Total, and the Burmese military junta.

One local activist told Redford how he and others had written to Unocal and to the U.S. government describing the violence they suffered. They received no response. The young man asked her: Given that he had been ignored in his peaceful attempts to prevent the destruction of his community—did he have the legal right to blow up the pipeline? Redford pointed out that she was only a second-year law student, but she guessed that no, that would be illegal. "And, in any case," she added, "it's really not a great idea."

The question did, however, make her think through the challenge of how to find suitable redress. At the time, it seemed impossible.

Redford met with an activist named Ka Hsaw Wa, who had been jailed and tortured in 1988 for his part in Burma's prodemocracy protests. While working secretly near Burmese army units, Ka Hsaw Wa agreed to smuggle Redford across the border, where, despite a bout of malaria, she gathered information for a report on the brutality connected with the pipeline.

Redford documented a range of horrific abuses. In one case a woman's baby was thrown into a fire and burned alive. As Redford later recalled: "Refugees who were literally fleeing their burned homes, fearing murder, rape, or being seized for forced labor, would look me in the eye and say, 'Please, when you go back to your country, use your freedom to protect ours. Use your rights to protect ours.'"

On returning to law school, Redford searched for a way to force Unocal to take responsibility for the abuses that she believed had been committed on Unocal's behalf. She focused especially on an obscure law signed by George Washington in 1789 and originally intended to combat piracy. Two centuries later, Redford believed the long-defunct Alien Tort Claims Act might have a useful role to play, by giving U.S. courts the jurisdiction to make rulings against companies in connection with international crimes committed against individuals outside the United States.

Redford worked for a year on a paper that explored those options. The paper gained her an academic A. But her professor assured her that she was deluded if she thought that suing an international oil company in connection with abuses in a far-off country could ever happen in the real world. Redford later described the conversation: "It will never happen. It's a terrible idea. You will not succeed."

Redford challenged that confident assessment. In 1995, she and Ka Hsaw Wa founded the nonprofit organization EarthRights International. Using the arguments first set out in her student paper, they filed suit on behalf of fifteen Burmese villagers in an unprecedented legal action as corporate America looked on nervously. Then, in a landmark decision in 1997, a federal district court in Los Angeles concluded that U.S. courts can adjudicate claims against corporations for complicity in abuses committed overseas.

A series of appeals and counterappeals followed. Finally, in December 2004, just months before the trial was due to begin, Unocal settled out of court. Though the amount has never officially been disclosed, the company is reported to have paid millions of dollars in compensation.

For those involved, as important as the money was the principle. A law student, and those she went on to work with, proved wrong those who believed that villagers on the other side of the world could never challenge a global company for its part in their suffering. As one of the forced-labor victims said, "I don't care about the money. Most of all I wanted the world to know what Unocal did. Now you know."

Redford and Ka Hsaw Wa, who were married in 1996, continue in their work with EarthRights International to highlight connections between human rights abuses and international business. Companies around the world—in Indonesia, Nigeria, and elsewhere—have been forced to think about their human rights responsibilities as never before.

Explosive Effects

Seen from today's perspective, it may seem obvious that there should be a global ban on the use of landmines. Overwhelmingly, the victims are not soldiers, but civilians maimed or killed many years after the conflict is over. Lethal activities include walking, playing, bicycling, or plowing a field. The very existence of landmines seems like an offense against humanity. And yet, when activists began to campaign for an international ban in the 1990s, they were dismissed as mere dreamers. In the words of *Banning Landmines,* an account published in 2008 by campaigners Jody Williams, Stephen Goose, and Mary Wareham, "The odds were very long, the obstacles immense, the process fragile and the outcome extremely uncertain throughout."

Politicians around the world argued that proposals for a ban were impractical. Australian foreign minister Gareth Evans (quoted in *Banning Landmines*) told the country's

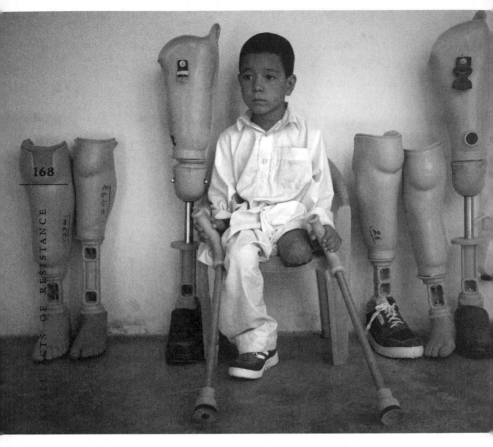

SMALL ACTS OF RESISTANCE

Herat, Afghanistan. Politicians insisted that, "in the real world," an international ban on landmines could never happen. Millions came together to prove the skeptics wrong.

Credit: UPI/Hossein Fatemi

Senate in June 1995 that the idea of a landmine ban was "hopelessly utopian." It would never happen in "the real world that the rest of us inhabit," he said. It was impossible "to argue with the military realities."

Others disagreed. In Cambodia alone, campaigners gathered more than 300,000 signatures for a ban. The International Campaign to Ban Landmines brought together more than 1,200 nongovernmental organizations from sixty countries. Six tons of shoes were delivered to government delegates at a conference in Austria as a reminder of the countless civilians who would never wear shoes again. In Italy, workers at a large landmine-producing factory called for a ban. In Geneva, delegates to a diplomatic conference were confronted by a clock that registered the growing death toll in real time—a new victim every twenty minutes.

Gradually, as casualties continued to mount, the diplomatic momentum grew. Canadian foreign minister Lloyd Axworthy piled on the pressure by announcing, at a meeting of governments in Ottawa in 1996 to discuss the proposals for a landmine ban, that Canada would host a treaty-signing conference the following year. Campaigners cheered. Most diplomats, unhappy that they no longer had excuses for inaction, did not.

In September 1997, a treaty banning landmines was agreed to in Oslo. In October, the International Campaign to Ban Landmines and its coordinator, Jody Williams, received the Nobel Peace Prize.

Two months later, as promised by Axworthy the previous year, the landmine treaty was signed in Canada. Australia and Cambodia were among the 120 countries that signed the treaty in Ottawa on December 3, 1997. Canadian prime minister Jean Chrétien described the signing as "the triumph of the forces of good in life."

At the time of this writing, 156 countries have become parties to the treaty. (Equally remarkable, a similar international coalition of nongovernmental organizations has, in the meantime, successfully pressed for a treaty banning the use of deadly cluster munitions—a ban that just a few years ago seemed unthinkable.) Holdouts who still refuse to sign the landmine treaty include the governments of China, Iran, North Korea, Russia—and the United States.

13

When Walls Come Tumbling Down

The most important moment, the moment that will determine
the fate of the country, the Shah and the revolution, is the
moment when one policeman walks from his post toward one
man on the edge of the crowd, raises his voice, and orders the
man to go home . . .

There is a moment of silence. We don't know whether the
policeman and the man on the edge of the crowd already realize
what has happened. The man has stopped being afraid—and
this is precisely the beginning of the revolution . . .

To appease the generals, [the Shah] ordered that the inhabitants
of Isfahan be fired on. The people responded with an outburst
of anger and hatred. He wanted to appease the people, so he
dismissed the head of Savak [the secret police]. Savak was
appalled. To appease Savak, the Shah allowed them to arrest
whomever they wished. And so by reversals, detours, meanderings,
and zigzags, step by step, he drew nearer to the precipice.

—Ryszard Kapuściński, *Shah of Shahs*,
on the Iranian revolution of 1979

The moment someone breaks through in one place, when one
person cries out: "The emperor is naked!"—everything appears in
another light.

—Václav Havel, *The Power of the Powerless* (1978)

171

Questions of Power

*Our natural tendency to place the possible in the past leads us
often to overlook the acts of our contemporaries, who defy the
presumably unmovable order of things, and accomplish what at
first sight has seemed impossible or improbable.*

—CZESŁAW MIŁOSZ, 1987

In spring 1989, the Hungarian Communist government was
eager to prove its newly liberal credentials, and therefore
organized a photo opportunity. On May 2, officials invited
journalists to watch the dismantling of part of the border
fence between Hungary and the West—thus chopping a
symbolic and literal hole in the Iron Curtain, which had
divided Europe for the previous four decades. Neighboring
hard-line Communist countries, especially East Germany,
were furious, but could do nothing.

Citizens of the repressive East German state were
allowed to travel to other Communist countries in eastern
Europe. Travel to the West, by contrast, was unthinkable. In
the months that followed, tens of thousands of East Germans
took advantage of their summer holidays in Hungary to
slip through the now-porous border between Hungary and
Austria, thus escaping the regime that had until then kept
them locked in, on pain of death.

One Hungarian group—ignoring the howls of indig-
nation from the authorities in East Berlin—even organized a
mass picnic on the border with Austria, attended by 20,000
people on August 19, 1989. East German vacationers came to
enjoy the picnic—and skipped off to the West after finishing
lunch. There was nothing that the Communist leadership in

East Germany could do, even as hundreds of thousands of its best and brightest streamed out of the country to the West in the weeks that followed.

The outpouring of East Germans via Hungary was dramatic enough. Meanwhile, even more problematic for the East German regime, vast crowds went out on the streets at home, chanting: "We are staying here!" That was not a declaration of loyalty. It meant: "We are staying because we are determined that everything in our country must change." Those who escaped across the border caused one kind of pressure, creating economic and political problems alike. But many of those who decided to stay behind were doing so because they were determined to ensure that their country changed, in a way that would make it worth living in at last.

Understandably, the authorities became increasingly worried, though the government felt it still possessed the ultimate trump card: violence.

Through the summer and autumn of 1989, protests—especially in the southern city of Leipzig—grew bigger week by week. The protests had begun as a weekly service of "prayers for peace" in the Nikolaikirche, a twelfth-century church in the heart of the city. Now, those weekly meetings had become huge protests, which spilled outside the church itself, with peaceful protest marches every Monday evening, demanding change. The authorities beat and arrested protesters. Still, though, the size of the Monday-night crowds continued to grow. The authorities decided: Enough was enough. A "letter to the editor" appeared in the local Leipzig paper on October

6, announcing that the protests would be firmly dealt with— "if need be, with weapons in our hands."

The letter purported to come from a concerned citizen. Leipzigers knew, however, that the supposed author of this letter was no ordinary newspaper reader. The letter contained, in effect, an official warning of the bloodshed that was yet to come. The idea was that the people should be too afraid to go out on the streets. Everyone knew about the deadly violence at Tiananmen Square in Beijing just four months earlier, which the East German authorities had publicly praised. This was no bluff.

As the church prayers before the intended protest march started up in the early evening of October 9, 1989, sixteen trucks with armed workers' militias stood waiting in one side street alone. Thousands of security forces were deployed. Foreign journalists were banned from the city. (As one of the authors of this book discovered, with luck it was possible to smuggle oneself into the city and avoid the authorities' unwanted attention; expulsion by the secret police came only later that night, after the demonstration was over.) Hospital wards were cleared, in expectation of casualties to come.

The impending threat of violence seemed like a good reason for everybody to stay at home. Instead, three times as many protesters came out on the streets as ever before, defying the threatened gunfire. (It was possible to witness a Leipzig pastor arguing in his apartment with his young daughter that day, forbidding her to go to the march that would begin a few hours later. He was allowed to die, ran the implied logic, but he would not allow his daughter to risk being killed.)

As seventy thousand demonstrators walked around the Leipzig inner ring road that evening, they waited fearfully for the shooting to begin. They chanted "No violence!" even as they braced for the gunfire. As was later confirmed, live ammunition had already been handed out to the security troops.

And then came the most astonishing event of all: Nothing happened. The government backed down from its decision to open fire, because, in the end, the authorities became too frightened of the crowds' lack of fear. They realized that the political cost of such bloodshed would be too high.

Gradually, as the protesters marched, the scale of the turnaround became clear. There would be no shooting this evening. There would not even be beatings or arrests, as there had been on all previous occasions. The well-armed, apparently invincible regime backed down at the last moment, because the unarmed crowds had not. This was, to quote the title of a 2009 documentary about the events of that day, *The Miracle of Leipzig*.

Demonstrators offered flowers and chatted to the militias who, just a few minutes earlier, had been expected to stage a historic bloodbath. This strangely glorious anticlimax was one of the most extraordinary moments in an extraordinary year. Anette Kiessner, hotel receptionist and one of the demonstrators, remembered afterwards, "I felt as if I could fly. It was the most fantastic day I have ever known. Now, we knew that there was no going back. October 3 [German unification, a year later, which marked the end of the East German state] was great. But October 9—that was the really special day."

The fall of the Berlin Wall came exactly a month later, on November 9, 1989. The victory in Leipzig became a victory for all East Germany—and thus for a changed world.

German unification followed within a year, transforming the face of Europe.

All the dramatic changes sweeping through eastern Europe in 1989 took place not because of the two superpowers, but above all because of ordinary people. Timothy Garton Ash, eyewitness of the revolutions and co-author of *Civil Resistance and Power Politics*, argues that the Soviet Union and the United States made history that year mostly by what they did *not* do: "And both giants stood back partly because they underestimated the significance of things being done by little people in little countries."

On October 9, 1989, seventy thousand people made the decision to go out on the streets, in the knowledge that they could expect to be shot at and might be killed. The courage of so many forced a previously unthinkable retreat.

Antidotes

I don't feel like being afraid, and that's an end of the matter. We've drunk the antidote. Fear, which poisoned us all our life, slowly but surely—like an ancient venom—did its job. It killed people. But freedom, which we greedily fell upon, killed fear within a few years. . . . In the long run, what can they do to us? Suppose they kill us. But we've already become free. They can't rob us of that.

—ALEXANDER KABAKOV, FEBRUARY 1991,
SIX MONTHS BEFORE UNARMED PROTESTERS
DEFEATED A COMMUNIST HARD-LINE COUP

In August 1968 when Russian tanks invaded Czechoslovakia to end the "Prague Spring"—liberalizing reforms by the

Czech government—Russians remained almost silent in the face of their own country's crimes. In Prague, huge crowds protested; in Moscow, almost nobody did.

Natalia Gorbanevskaya, a thirty-two-year-old Russian poet, was one of just seven Russians to protest their government's action, in Red Square in Moscow on August 25, 1968. All seven were jailed, sent to labor camps, or—in Gorbanevskaya's case—committed to a closed psychiatric hospital for life.

At the time, it seemed that those seven people had made not the tiniest dent in the might of the Soviet Union. But, as dissident Anatoli Yakobson predicted at the time, the impact of the Red Square protest would go far beyond its miniature size. "All those in our country who seek the truth have heard of the demonstration; so have the people of Czechoslovakia; so has humanity at large. The importance of the demonstration on August 25 cannot be overstated," he wrote in *Red Square at Noon,* a book published abroad that described the small and courageous act of protest on that day.

Yakobson was proved right. Gorbanevskaya and her colleagues set an extraordinary example. In the years to come, seven Russian protesters against repression became seventy. Seventy became seven hundred. Seven hundred became seven thousand and seventy thousand and more.

Some of the country's Communist leaders, meanwhile, failed to understand how much their own country had changed during those years. Beginning in the early hours of Monday, August 19, 1991—twenty-three years after Gorbanevskaya's small protest—members of the ruling Politburo staged a coup, announcing that the reformist leader Mikhail Gorbachev had been removed from his post for "health reasons." Gorbachev was locked incommunicado in his holiday villa in the Crimea, and the coup organizers put tanks on the streets of Moscow to end all prospect of further change.

Western politicians were convinced that this meant that all Gorbachev's reforms were now over. Some even began to deal with the coup leaders. But ordinary Russians decided differently. Crowds gathered to protest against the unwanted takeover. An illegally published and widely distributed newspaper declared, "The coup is only strong if we are afraid." The mayor of Leningrad threatened that coup supporters in the city would be put on trial "like the Nazis were at Nuremberg" (it was a bluff, but it worked). Fear was no longer all-pervasive. Many Russians had indeed, as writer Alexander Kabakov had argued a few months earlier, "drunk the antidote."

The coup plotters did their best to keep a lid on things, even as crowds came out onto the streets to defend all the changes that had been achieved, and to push for more. Russian state television broadcast endless reruns of Tchaikovsky ballet performances, apparently intended as a political tranquilizer. (A military officer later complained, "Could it happen in any civilized country that the army takes over, and all the people get is *Swan Lake?*")

The crowds grew and grew. On Tuesday, August 20, barely twenty-four hours after the coup began, 100,000 gathered in central Moscow, ready to oppose the tanks with their lives. Some troops came over to the protesters' side, where they were treated as heroes. ("No, really!" said one soldier as an old woman pressed him to take yet another home-baked pie, which she, like others, had brought with her as a kind of peace offering for the young conscripts. "I can't eat any more.")

The coup leaders were ready to use lethal violence, if need be. On Tuesday night, three people died—by shooting, and under the tracks of military vehicles. Still, though, the crowds refused to back down. Instead, they successfully blockaded armored personnel carriers with trolley buses and a street-cleaning truck. Trapped soldiers fled.

A KGB officer who spent that night at the secret police headquarters in central Moscow later described the mood. Those who had been so determined to suppress all freedoms gradually understood that it was they, not those who were defying the regime, who were about to lose, despite all the guns and tanks at their disposal. In the KGB man's words, "Many, especially those who had been so happy at the beginning, looked depressed and their eyes showed a presentiment of evil, as a dog does just before an earthquake. The dogs know something very bad is coming soon, but cannot understand quite what it will be."

Soon, it became clear just how bad things had become for the men with all the guns. At around midday on Wednesday, August 21, the coup plotters all piled into their limousines and headed for the airport. The coup had collapsed in less than three days because hundreds of thousands of peaceful protesters were ready to risk their lives to defeat it.

With reference to the nonstop reruns of *Swan Lake,* a popular badge after the coup showed coup plotter and former defense minister General Dmitry Yazov dressed as a ballet dancer. The general's speech bubble demanded: "Everybody,

DANCE!" But Russians had refused to dance to his tune. Four months after the failed coup, the one-party Soviet Union itself—sustained by tanks and repression for more than seventy years—officially ceased to exist.

14

The Power of One

No snowflake in an avalanche ever feels responsible.
—Stanisław Lec

Unwanted Heroes

Raoul Wallenberg, a Swedish diplomat, saved tens of thousands of Jews in the Hungarian capital, Budapest, during the Second World War before he was captured by the Russians (who claimed he was a spy) and never seen again. His name is well-known. For decades, he has been internationally lauded for his heroism.

Carl Lutz, a Swiss diplomat, also saved tens of thousands of Jews in Budapest, and took enormous risks to do so. He is scarcely known. During his lifetime, he was ignored or ostracized.

Lutz's lifesaving acts were certainly remarkable. Acting on his own initiative, Lutz created a fictional emigration department of the Swiss Legation, and ordered a brass plaque with that name to be engraved and displayed. He opened dozens of safe houses, each of which he claimed were attached to the Swiss diplomatic mission, and thus were sovereign Swiss territory, enjoying diplomatic immunity. A glass merchant's house at 29 Vadász Street in Budapest, known as the Glass House because it was almost entirely covered in windows, became the headquarters of the spurious new department.

The Germans reluctantly agreed to recognize 8,000 of Lutz's "protection letters" for Hungarian Jews. For Lutz, that was not enough. He deliberately misinterpreted the agreement to mean families, not just individuals—and he secretly told his staff to produce far more than the 8,000 letters that he was authorized to issue. He told them to issue up to 100,000 protection letters—because that was the number of Jews the Nazis wanted to deport to the camps. A witness, quoted in Theo Tschuy's biography of Lutz, *Dangerous Diplomacy*, described the scene outside the Glass House in late 1944: "People line up by the thousands to obtain the miraculous paper. And indeed the paper is miraculous. . . . Each single paper means a human being saved." In total, Lutz rescued an astonishing 60,000 Jews in this way.

Lutz and Wallenberg cooperated closely, and the parallels between their work are clear. Indeed, Lutz encouraged Wallenberg to take up his lifesaving work. Shortly after the Swedish diplomat arrived in Budapest in July 1944, it was Lutz who explained to him the extent of the crisis, and the urgent need to save thousands of lives.

The differences in their reputations are, however, equally striking. Wallenberg, who was arrested by the Russians in 1945 and apparently disappeared into the labor camps of Siberia, was an obviously acceptable candidate to be an international hero, not least because the mystery surrounding his disappearance and the unknown date of his death helped foster a wide-ranging Wallenberg mythology.

Lutz's superiors, by contrast, ordered an investigation when he returned home in 1945 into why he had flouted orders by saving so many people when he had no instructions to do so. The judge cleared him, and even scolded the government for launching the investigation. Lutz was allowed to remain a diplomat. But, during his lifetime at least, he received no official apology.

Nor was it just the Swiss who were unhappy with Lutz's wartime actions. Neutral Switzerland was responsible for representing British interests in occupied Budapest. The British government rebuked Lutz for his lifesaving obstinacy. One British diplomat reinforced the instructions to Lutz not to save so many lives (which would put pressure on Britain's own immigration policies) with angry, multiple underlining in a note written in 1944, when the Holocaust was at its height: "5000 = five thousand individuals, not families (!)"

Lutz died in obscurity in 1975. Twenty years after his death and fifty years after his unrewarded courage, he was acknowledged as a hero. In 1995, the Swiss government declared the disobedient diplomat to be one of the outstanding citizens in the country's history.

There is much we could have done to save the Jews of Europe before the war. There is much we could have done since the war began. There are still things we could do today which would give new lives to a few and hope to many. . . . There are people who say the President cannot risk [allowing Jewish refugees into the United States] before election. I believe that is an insult to the American people . . . It is a question of courage and good faith.
—I. F. STONE IN *The Nation*, JUNE 10, 1944

Varian Fry, a thirty-two-year-old American journalist, arrived in the French port of Marseille in 1940. His mission, on behalf of what later came to be known as the International Rescue Committee, was to help those fleeing the Nazis to reach safety in the United States. Fry's achievements were impressive—too impressive, as far as the U.S. government was concerned. Initially, Fry was able to arrange special U.S. "emergency visitor's visas" for those he helped to smuggle across the Pyrenees out of Nazi-occupied France into Spain and Portugal, and from there across the Atlantic. But, as

Sheila Isenberg describes in *A Hero of Our Own*, that did not last. Hiram Bingham IV, U.S. vice-consul in Marseille who supported Fry's work and helped him with visas, was relieved of his post in 1941. Breckinridge Long, assistant secretary of state, was responsible for immigration issues, and wanted officials to "put every obstacle in the way" in order to "postpone and postpone and postpone the granting of the visas." Long preferred a policy of "America for the Americans." The last thing that officials wanted was for a busybody like Fry to help *more* people gain a chance of reaching American shores—with or without a visa, with or without valid documents.

In June 1941, the U.S. consulate ordered Fry to leave France once and for all. He was told that his expiring passport would not be renewed until he returned to the United States. When Fry arrived home, he was refused a new passport, and his mail was censored.

When Varian Fry died in 1967, his work was still unrecognized. Three decades after his death, Fry was honored at Israel's Holocaust memorial, Yad Vashem. U.S. Secretary of State Warren Christopher admitted on that occasion, with some understatement, "His heroic actions never received the support they deserved."

"Ordinary Things"

Rwanda was a failure on so many levels ... It was a failure of Western democracies to step in and avert the catastrophe when abundant evidence was available. It was a failure of the United States for not calling a genocide by its right name. It was the failure of the United Nations to live up to its commitments as a peacemaking body.

All of these come down to a failure of words. And this is what I want to tell you: Words are the most effective weapons of death in man's arsenal. But they can also be powerful tools of life . . . Today I am convinced that the only thing that saved those 1,268 people in my hotel was words. Not the liquor, not money, not the UN. Just ordinary words directed against the darkness.

—PAUL RUSESABAGINA, MANAGER OF THE

MILLE COLLINES HOTEL IN RWANDA IN 1994

The eighteenth-century philosopher Edmund Burke wrote, "All that is necessary for the triumph of evil is for good men to do nothing." In Rwanda, he was proved right. When a well-orchestrated, premeditated genocide began on April 6, 1994, the world's politicians did nothing. That failure made it possible for evil to triumph. Hutu extremists slaughtered 800,000 Tutsis and independent-minded Hutus in just three months, while powerful governments looked the other way.

One Rwandan single-handedly saved 1,268 men, women, and children from the Hutu killers during those months. Paul Rusesabagina, manager of the Mille Collines Hotel (whose story was later told in the film *Hotel Rwanda*), challenged the killers many times over, each time risking his life by doing so. Despite all the dangers, Rusesabagina insisted in his memoir, *An Ordinary Man:* "There was nothing particularly heroic about it . . . I did what I believed to be the ordinary things that an ordinary man would do."

The courage of Rusesabagina and others was never matched by international resolve. Instead, foreigners who wanted to address the problem were repeatedly slapped down. Three months before the genocide began, Roméo Dallaire, Canadian commander of the UN force in Rwanda, learned of secret arms caches and death lists in the Rwandan capital, Kigali. Dallaire cabled United Nations headquarters in New York about his intentions to seize the weapons, and thus head off the murderous conspiracy that was being hatched. His message of January 11, 1994 ended on an upbeat note. *"Peux ce que veux. Allons-y!"*—"Where there's a will, there's a way. Let's go!" In New York, there was no will, and therefore no way. Dallaire was forbidden to act. He protested and was rebuffed.

When the mass killing began, those who cared most about Rwanda were not surprised. Rwandan activist Monique Mujawamariya had written of the threat of "an instantaneous, carefully prepared operation" even before the genocide began. Mujawamariya hung up the phone on her friend Alison Des Forges from Human Rights Watch as the killers knocked at her door on the first day. She told Des Forges (who later wrote *Leave None to Tell the Story*, the definitive account of the genocide), "Please take care of my children. I don't want you to hear this." Mujawamariya—whom Bill Clinton had told, four months before the genocide began: "Your courage is an inspiration to all of us"—survived by a miracle after hiding in the roof. She escaped Rwanda to tell her story and the story of the unfolding genocide. But the politicians refused to listen. Humanitarian organizations on the ground, like Oxfam and Médecins Sans Frontières (Doctors without Borders), repeatedly sounded the alarm. Still, though, the politicians remained deaf to the calls for action.

Powerful governments even rebuked those smaller members of the UN Security Council, like the Czech Republic and New Zealand, which had the gall to speak out. The British ambassador told his Czech colleague that the Security Council would become "a laughingstock" if it talked of genocide. As described in Samantha Power's Pulitzer Prize–winning *A Problem from Hell*, the United States administration forbade officials to admit that this was genocide, in case America might then feel obliged to save lives. The State Department began what Power described as "a two-month dance to avoid the g-word." France went still further, hosting politicians who were themselves responsible for mass murder.

Hate radio formed a central part of the planning of the genocide. Radio broadcasts directed the killers in real time, urging the killing of Tutsi "cockroaches." The jamming of hate radio broadcasts, it is generally acknowledged, would have sent a strong signal—and could have saved lives. The Pentagon decreed, however, in a memo prepared a month into the genocide, that the jamming would be too expensive. The cost would have been $8,500 an hour. That was deemed to be too high a price for potentially saving a few hundred thousand lives.

With his courage and his words alone, Rusesabagina saved many lives. Countless other Rwandans risked their lives to save friends and neighbors. Each act of kindness would have cost the rescuer his or her own life, if discovered. Dallaire and his small United Nations force saved lives, too, despite the lack of support from New York. Dallaire, praised by Rwandans for what he tried to do, suffered a nervous collapse a few years later over what he had been through. (He later wrote an award-winning memoir, *Shake Hands with the Devil: The Failure of Humanity in Rwanda*.)

As with the Milgram experiment thirty years earlier, however (involving electric shocks and moral backbone,

Chapter 7), those who had much to feel guilty about seemed especially eager to find others to blame. President Bill Clinton provided a half-apology for his government's determination to look away from Rwanda's suffering. The president—with an interesting interpretation of the phrase *The buck stops here*—blamed the failures, however, not on himself but on "the people that were bringing these decisions to me."

Calling Evil by Its Name

It began with the trial in 1921 of a young Armenian, Soghomon Tehlirian, prosecuted for the assassination of the Turkish interior minister, Talaat Pasha. Raphael Lemkin, a twenty-one-year-old Polish-Jewish law student, could not understand why Tehlirian could be prosecuted, while the Turkish interior minister—who was responsible for the deaths of hundreds of thousands of Armenian civilians in forced marches and massacres in 1915—could not. Lemkin asked his law professor why it was a crime for somebody "to kill one man, but not a crime for his oppressor to kill more than a million men." Lemkin concluded, "This is most inconsistent."

Twenty years later, as Hitler launched his campaign of annihilation, the idea that entire populations could be murdered without consequences clearly needed addressing more urgently than ever. (Hitler himself pointed out to his colleagues that it was easy to get away with mass murder. "Who remembers the Armenians now?" he asked.)

In October 1939, a month after Hitler's invasion of Poland, Lemkin escaped from Poland to Sweden. Two years later he arrived in the United States, and took up a teaching post at Duke University in North Carolina. While there, he worked on the ideas that had troubled him for two decades. In 1943, he published *Axis Rule in Europe,* a seven-hundred-page treatise on Hitler's killing machine in eastern Europe, which included "proposals for redress." Lemkin believed that it was essential to come up with a single, memorable name to identify the still unnamed crime. The word *homicide* describes the killing of a person. *Infanticide* refers to the killing of a child. Taking the Greek word for race or tribe, *genos,* Lemkin proposed a new word: *genocide.*

The word quickly took hold. Even after 1945, however, many governments refused to accept that there was any need to outlaw genocide. Lemkin continued to fight on relentlessly, in a one-man diplomatic struggle—a pure obsession. Because of Lemkin's determination, a treaty outlawing genocide was—remarkably—adopted by governments at the United Nations in 1948.

Even then, however, the mere existence of a piece of paper changed nothing on the ground. Lemkin's biographer, John Cooper, quotes one of Lemkin's former law students, who wrote to him in 1951 that his achievements would only be recognized in the years to come: "It is true that you cannot see the results of your work. But your work is great, far greater than this generation."

Lemkin died in 1959. Seven people attended his funeral. But Lemkin's student was right to take a longer perspective on his work. Ninety years after Lemkin's argument with his law professor, genocide is finally being confronted, in part as a result of his work.

In the final years of the twentieth century and the early years of the twenty-first, there have been prosecutions and convictions for crimes against humanity and genocide in

Bosnia, Cambodia, Iraq, Rwanda, and elsewhere. In 2009, the newly created International Criminal Court, which came into existence in 2002, indicted the Sudanese president Omar al-Bashir for the deaths of hundreds of thousands of civilians in Darfur. Half a century after the obsessive Lemkin's death, his impact is felt more strongly than ever before.

15

Digital Dissent

You see, wire telegraph is a kind of a very, very long cat. You pull his tail in New York and his head is meowing in Los Angeles. Do you understand this? And radio operates exactly the same way: You send signals here, they receive them there. The only difference is that there is no cat.

—Albert Einstein, explaining the mysteries of modern communication

There is no reason anyone would want a computer in their home.

—Ken Olsen, president of Digital Equipment Corporation, 1977

Tehran, June 2009.

Twitterithmetic

Whose hand but yours and mine can pull back these curtains.

—FROM THE IRANIAN SONG "YARE DABESTANI," QUOTED BY SHIRIN EBADI IN *Iran Awakening: A Memoir of Rebellion and Hope*

In advance of the Iranian presidential elections of June 2009, opinion polls showed a clear majority for the opposition candidate Mir-Hossein Moussavi. When the authorities announced that the hard-line president, Mahmoud Ahmadinejad, had been reelected by a 2–1 landslide, millions of Iranian voters thought differently.

Hundreds of thousands—young and old, women and men, manual laborers and middle-class—went out on the streets, defying the violence of the officially sponsored *basij* vigilantes. Out of reach of the *basij*, Iranians gathered on the rooftops of apartment buildings, chanting, *"Allahu akbar"* ("God is great") and "Death to the dictator!"—slogans last heard during the revolution that led to the fall of the Shah three decades earlier.

The regime was furious that Iranians dared speak out. The authorities partly shut down phone texting, along with Facebook and other social networking sites. Foreign journalists were thrown out of the country. Those who remained were forbidden to report from the streets.

Despite all the restrictions, however, information still got out—to Iranians and to the rest of the world. At one point, the BBC Persian Service was receiving material from inside Iran at the rate of five videos a minute. Even the limited access to the Internet—including Twitter, and backdoor routes to Facebook and other websites—yielded a constant stream of information.

Twitter proved especially agile. The 140-character tweets from the street enabled protesters to share information in real time, hundreds of thousands an hour, with news updates and advice on how to defy the Internet restrictions: "Advice— your location can be identified from mobile signal + delete all SMS [text messages] after sending in case u are arrested," or "Protest with the Koran in your hand, sit down if they attack, while citing the Koran 8.61, use Gandhi method."

President Ahmadinejad was inaugurated, despite the continuing protests. But many Iranians believe that those vast tweet- and text-message-fueled demonstrations mean that Iran will never be the same again.

Texting for Justice

Text messaging may seem like an unusual way of achieving justice, but that is what happened in India in 2006.

In 1999, model Jessica Lal was shot dead in a crowded Delhi bar filled with moneyed customers. There were witnesses, and police were present at the scene. But witnesses retracted their testimony. Evidence vanished. Manu Sharma—who had initially confessed to the killing—was acquitted, as were eight others who stood accused of destroying evidence.

Sharma's father was a wealthy politician. Many Indians believed Sharma's acquittal confirmed that the rich and powerful were above the law. The NDTV television news channel launched a campaign calling for justice. Anchor Barkha Dutt said, "There comes a time in the life of every society, of every country when one person's story touches something in all of us." The station called on viewers to send text messages in a mass digital petition. In just three days, NDTV received more than 200,000 such messages.

The response resonated across the country. Many saw evidence of a sea change in Indian middle-class attitudes, which, until then, seemed resigned to the corruption in the system. It was as if justice for Lal could help win justice for others in the future. Evidence emerged that witnesses had been bribed. The pressure became overwhelming for the prosecution's appeal to be heard.

On December 15, 2006, the Indian High Court found Sharma guilty on existing evidence. He was sentenced to life imprisonment.

Powerful Underwear

When supporters of the Hindu nationalist Sri Ram Sena (SRS) organization attacked a group of women in Mangalore in southern India for the crime of sitting in the pub, they met a reaction they could never have expected. An entire protest movement mobilized via Facebook to confront the nationalists—with the help of thousands of pairs of pink underwear.

The attack on the women was part of a nationalist campaign in 2009 to "protect" Indian culture. For the SRS, this meant opposing dangerous foreign influences, which included everything from pubgoing to the celebration of Valentine's Day. Any unmarried couple seen in public on February 14 would be forced to marry, the SRS declared.

The SRS demand that nobody should celebrate Valentine's Day may have seemed absurd. But the underlying threat of violence was real—not just in connection with Valentine's Day, but against all women who seek to make choices of their own.

Journalist Nisha Susan decided to take action against the nationalists' attempts to dictate what women could and could not choose to do. She started a Facebook group called the Consortium of Pub-going, Loose and Forward Women. The Consortium called on women across India to celebrate Valentine's Day with a mild act of defiance: "Walk to the nearest pub and buy a drink. Raise a toast to the Sri Ram Sena." The group gained thirty thousand supporters within a week.

As Susan pointed out, "For many of those who signed up, neither Valentine's Day nor pubgoing meant anything. What we agreed on is the need to end violence in the name of somebody's idea of Indian culture."

Thousands heeded the Facebook call to send "pink chaddis"—a colloquial word for underwear—to the leader of the SRS, Pramod Muthalik. The pink chaddis campaign infuriated Muthalik and his fellow zealots—and provided an opportunity for a powerful expression of solidarity against the violence.

On the consortium's Facebook page, a message appeared after the protests were over: "Valentine's Day has come and gone. Chaddis have been sent and burnt. Trolls have danced a few dances. We are still around. We still say nyaah to moral policing. We still say nyaah to bullies."

Colts Untamed

The authorities consider the technology as a "wild colt" that must be tamed, but we independent bloggers want the wild colt to run freely. The difficulties of disseminating our sites are many. From hand to hand—thanks to flash drives, CDs, and obsolete diskettes—the content of blogs travels the island . . . Now is the time for us to jump the wall of control.

—Yoani Sánchez, Cuban blogger

The 2009 Havana Biennial Festival of Contemporary Art contained many works that sought to provoke the Cuban regime. None more so than the performance organized by artist Tania Bruguera, who took public impudence to a new level.

In Castro's Cuba—first under Fidel Castro, and then under his brother Raúl—those who dare to speak out against the government have frequently received long jail sentences. Bruguera confronted that repression head-on. She arranged for a podium with a microphone and encouraged her fellow Cubans to come up and say whatever they wanted, for up to one minute each. Actors dressed in military fatigues flanked the podium. An unruly, fluttering dove was placed on the shoulder of whoever chose to speak.

There were gasps of surprise as one speaker after another came to the microphone to protest the lack of basic freedoms—like blogger Yoani Sánchez, who called for Cubans to "jump the wall of control." One man declared: "I'm twenty. It's the first time I have felt so free." He called on older people to speak out. There were repeated cries from the floor of *Libertad!* and *Bravo!* "Too many years of covering the sun with one finger!" said one man.

In a country where all public protests are strictly banned, Bruguera's artistic happening was an extraordinary event. It may well have become a talking point in Havana and across the country, even if only the few hundred people in the room had witnessed it. But the performance was taped and posted on YouTube. It became an immediate hit—including by those who passed it around on flash drives because of the difficulties with Cuban access to the Internet.

The authorities were unhappy. The festival's organizing committee complained that the performance was "an anticultural event of shameful opportunism."

Yoani Sánchez, whose unauthorized blog, Generation Y, was named by *Time* magazine as one of the most important blogs of 2009, saw it differently. She rejoiced not just at the performance, but also at the official diatribe that followed. Without the diatribe, Sánchez said, the performance "would have seemed like something fabricated to give the appearance of openness."

As it was, the official attack on Bruguera's event gave the performance additional legitimacy. "With their accusations, they have exposed the reason why so many didn't dare—that night—to take the microphone," said Sánchez.

Cuddly Subversion

As for what you can and cannot watch, watch what you can watch, and don't watch what you cannot watch.

—Chinese foreign ministry spokesman Qin Gang explains the rules concerning the Internet, March 31, 2009

In China, the Internet is heavily censored. Websites that tell uncomfortable truths are blocked, and search engines are strangely unhelpful if you search for, say, "Tiananmen massacre," with reference to the slaughter of peaceful protesters in June 1989. Messages vary from "Sorry, we have found nothing relating to your request" to unrelated search results, which have nothing to do with the killings of June 1989. The Great Firewall of China, as it has come to be known, seeks to ensure that views alternative or challenging to those of the government cannot be heard.

In that context, the sudden popularity in 2009 of videos about an alpacalike animal known as the grass-mud horse, with Disneyish songs providing the musical sound track, does not sound subversive. But the sudden vogue for alpaca look-alikes left the Chinese authorities both unsettled and enraged.

Millions of delighted Chinese watched the grass-mud horse videos. Cuddly grass-mud horse toys became popular. And the government was furious.

The trouble was all in a name. When the word for the grass-mud horse—in Chinese, *caonima*—is pronounced, it sounds almost identical to an obscene and insulting phrase. (Imagine if there were an exotic animal known in English as a *fakkyamava*, and you have a close translation.) For the bloggers and Internet posters, the videos and songs were an opportunity to go rebelliously wild—and, with luck, unpunished.

It might seem as though this were mere child's play—fooling with childish songs that hinted at profanity. For the Chinese, though, the craze for the *fakkyamavas* was more than that. The grass-mud horses were a chance to thumb your nose at the censor, while pretending not to. Millions of Chinese rejoiced at the YouTube videos of scampering *fakkyamavas,* whose accompanying songs flirted not just with vulgarity but with the unspeakable in politics, too.

The *fakkyamavas* have a problem that blights their life— *river crabs,* a word that in Chinese sounds almost identical to the word for *harmony. Harmonizing* is a popular Chinese euphemism for official censorship. In short: The greatest enemies of the gamboling grass-mud horses are the censors, whom the grass-mud horses eventually defeat. In the words of one YouTube song:

> Oh lying down grass-mud horse,
>
> Oh running wild grass-mud horse,
>
> They defeated river crabs in order to protect their grassland
>
> River crabs forever disappeared . . .

The mockery only served to enrage China's outfoxed censors more than ever.

Commentators around the world sometimes suggest that ordinary Chinese no longer think about such long-forgotten events as the 1989 massacre in Tiananmen Square, and that students are now more interested in other matters than politics. As a professor at Peking University told the *New York Times*: "They think about their personal affairs, how to get a job, how to go abroad." The new economic opportunities for millions of Chinese give plenty of reasons not to think too much about public protest.

And yet, in the immediate runup to the twentieth anniversary, the authorities closed down access to a number of Internet services—including Twitter, the photo-sharing site Flickr, and popular search engines. The regime, in other words, seemed unconvinced that everybody had forgotten about the events of 1989.

Zhou Enlai, Chinese prime minister for three decades, famously noted that it takes a long time before one can see historic events fully in perspective. In the 1970s, he was asked to comment on the impact of the French Revolution two centuries earlier. He reportedly answered: "It's too early to tell."

Perhaps Zhou was right. Certainly, historical impact is hard to measure in the space of just a few years. Nobody can be sure whether Charter 08—a prodemocracy document signed by thousands of Chinese intellectuals in 2008—will prove to be a mere historical footnote or a milestone.

The signatories of Charter 08 deliberately risked jail by putting their names on the document, which calls freedom, equality, and human rights "universal common values shared by all humankind."

Seen from today's perspective, it seems unlikely that the impact of Charter 08 will be so dramatic as to make it possible to read an honest account of the Tiananmen massacre in an official Chinese newspaper any time soon. But the courageous signatories of Charter 08 (and the grass-mud horses battling with the river crabs) believe that today's situation cannot last forever. In their words: "Change is no longer optional."

Kathmandu, Nepal, January 2006. "They are the ones who are afraid the most."
Credit: Paula Bronstein/Getty Images

In Conclusion

you were so small
compared to them, who always stood above
you, on steps, rostrums, platforms,
and yet it is enough for just one instant to stop
being afraid, or let's say
begin to be a little less afraid,
to become convinced that they are the ones,
that they are the ones who are afraid the most

— Stanisław Barańczak

There is no shortage of wrongs in the world. In repressive contexts around the globe, it is always possible to find persuasive reasons why regimes are unlikely to change their ways. Those who see themselves as "realists" argue that confronting powerful rulers is therefore a futile waste of time.

However, some people are brave or deluded enough to believe that they can change things, and right wrongs, if enough people only believe that change is possible. They think change is worth taking risks for—even when there is no certainty of the outcome.

Those are the people who have made extraordinary change possible in the past. And those are the people who will achieve change in the years to come—through acts of resistance large and small.

When something is called impossible, it becomes so. Fear of consequences—not just fear of repression, but fear of ridicule or failure—leads to a reluctance to act. When that fear is put to one side (if only for a moment), previously unthinkable possibilities open up. Stanisław Barańczak, as quoted on page 209, has been proven right.

Not just in his native Poland (where, as described in this book, baby strollers and illegal ketchup helped bring about extraordinary change) but around the world.

Somewhere in the world, every day, some of those who have suffered begin to be less afraid, and some of those who have caused suffering begin to be more afraid of the change that may yet come.

Small acts of resistance continue. History has shown us that it is impossible to believe too much in the power of change.

Acknowledgments

We could never have written this book without the help of countless friends and colleagues who provided ideas, encouragement, comments, and advice.

Steve would especially like to thank Bashair Ahmed, Maureen Aung-thwin, Leeam Azulay-Yagev, Nicholas Bequelin, Reed Brody, Widney Brown, John Carlin, Emma Daly, Lucas Delattre, Boris Dittrich, Corinne Dufka, Hadi Ghaemi, Eduardo Gonzalez, Souleymane Guengueng, Peggy Hicks, Isabel Hilton, Tiseke Kasambala, Grzegorz Linkowski, Tanya Lokshina, Andrew Marshall, Juan Mendez, Lisa Misol, Marianne Møllmann, Anna Neistat, Tom Porteous, Sophie Richardson, James Ross, Rania Suidan, Stacy Sullivan, Wilder Tayler, Anneke Van Woudenberg, Mary Wareham, Minky Worden, and Sam Zia-Zarifi.

John would like to thank Tricia Duffield, Nic Dunlop, Lara Frank, Konstanty Gebert, Phillip Howze, Nina Jafferji, Shoka Javadiangilani, Yvette Mahon, Samantha Marshall, Michael Taylor, Radha Wickremasinghe, and Ko Aung Zaw.

Both of us owe thanks to three people who believed passionately in this book from the start, and thus made it happen—Carol Mann, Myrsini Stephanides, and Iris Blasi.

Thanks, too, for the enthusiasm and professionalism of the team at Sterling, which made the collaboration a pleasure throughout.

And, finally, a small disclaimer. This is, above all, a personal book for both authors. None of the opinions expressed should be taken to represent the views of any of the organizations with which we are or have been associated.

ACKNOWLEDGMENTS

Bibliography

Ackerman, Peter, and Jack DuVall. *A Force More Powerful: A Century of Nonviolent Conflict.* New York: Palgrave, 2000.

Arsenault, Raymond. *Freedom Riders: 1961 and the Struggle for Racial Justice.* New York: Oxford University Press, 2006.

———. *The Sound of Freedom: Marian Anderson, the Lincoln Memorial, and the Concert That Awakened America.* New York: Bloomsbury Books, 2009.

Aung San Suu Kyi. *Freedom from Fear and Other Writings.* London: Viking, 1991.

Banerjee, Mukilika. *The Pathan Unarmed.* Oxford, UK: Oxford University Press, 2000.

Bao Pu, ed. *Prisoner of the State: The Secret Journal of Premier Zhao Ziyang.* New York: Simon & Schuster, 2009.

Barańczak, Stanislaw. *Selected Poems: The Weight of the Body.* Chicago: Another Chicago Press, 1989.

Bichlbaum, Andy, and Mike Bonanno (directors). *The Yes Men Fix the World*, 2009.

Brecht, Bertolt. *Poems 1931–56.* New York: Routledge, 1997.

Cameron, Maxwell A., Robert J. Lawson, and Brian W. Tomlin. *To Walk without Fear: The Global Movement to Ban Landmines.* Toronto: Oxford University Press, 1998.

Carlin, John. *Playing the Enemy: Nelson Mandela and the Game that Made a Nation.* New York: Penguin, 2008.

Collin, Matthew. *This is Serbia Calling: Rock 'N' Roll Radio and Belgrade's Underground Resistance.* London: Serpent's Tail, 2001.

Cooper, John. *Raphael Lemkin and the Struggle for the Genocide Convention.* New York: Palgrave Macmillan, 2008.

Crawshaw, Steve (reporter), and Ian Taylor (director). "Estonian Revolution." Channel Four Television (UK), 1989.

Crawshaw, Steve. *Goodbye to the USSR: The Collapse of Soviet Power.* London: Bloomsbury, 1992.

———. *Easier Fatherland: Germany and the Twenty-First Century.* London: Continuum, 2004.

Dallaire, Roméo. *Shake Hands with the Devil: The Failure of Humanity in Rwanda.* New York: Carroll & Graf, 2003.

Delattre, Lucas. *A Spy at the Heart of the Third Reich: The Extraordinary Story of Fritz Kolbe, America's Most Important Spy in World War II.* New York: Atlantic Monthly Press, 2005.

Des Forges, Alison. *Leave None to Tell the Story: Genocide in Rwanda.* New York: Human Rights Watch/FIDH, 1999.

Dimeo, Paul, and James Mills, eds. *Soccer in South Asia: Empire, Nation, Diaspora.* London: Frank Cass Publishers, 2001.

Easwaran, Eknath. *Nonviolent Soldier of Islam: Badshah Khan, A Man to Match His Mountains.* Tomales, California: Blue Mountain Center of Meditation, 1999.

Ebadi, Shirin (with Azadeh Moaveni). *Iran Awakening: A Memoir of Revolution and Hope.* New York: Random House, 2006.

Fenton, James. *The Snap Revolution.* Cambridge, UK: Granta Publications, 1986.

Gorbanevskaya, Natalia. *Red Square at Noon.* London: André Deutsch, 1972.

Halberstam, David. *The Children.* New York: Random House, 1998.

Hallie, Philip. *Lest Innocent Blood Be Shed: The Story of the Village of Le Chambon and How Goodness Happened There.* New York: Harper & Row, 1979.

Havel, Václav. *Living in Truth.* London: Faber & Faber, 1987.

Hoose, Phillip. *Claudette Colvin: Twice Toward Justice.* New York: Farrar, Straus Giroux, 2009.

Isenberg, Sheila. *A Hero of Our Own: The Story of Varian Fry.* New York: Random House, 2001.

Joya, Malalai. *A Woman Among Warlords: The Extraordinary Story of an Afghan Who Dared to Raise Her Voice.* New York: Scribner Book Company, 2009.

Kapuściński, Ryszard. *Shah of Shahs.* London: Picador, 1986.

King, Mary Elizabeth. *A Quiet Revolution: The First Palestinian Intifada and Nonviolent Resistance.* New York: Nation Books, 2007.

Kidron, Peretz, ed. *Refusenik! Israel's Soldiers of Conscience.* London: Zed Books, 2004.

Korr, Chuck, and Marvin Close. *More Than Just a Game: Football v Apartheid.* London: Collins, 2008.

Kurlansky, Mark. *Nonviolence: Twenty-Five Lessons from the History of a Dangerous Idea.* New York: The Modern Library, 2006.

Kurspahić, Kemal. *As Long as Sarajevo Exists*. Stony Creek, Connecticut: The Pamphleteer's Press, 1997.

Lamptey, Comfort, et al., eds. *Liberian Women Peacemakers: Fighting for the Right to be Seen, Heard and Counted.* Trenton, New Jersey: Africa World Press, 2004.

Lewis, John. *Walking with the Wind: A Memoir of the Movement.* New York: Simon & Schuster, 1998.

Linkowski, Grzegorz (director), *Spacer z dziennikiem* ["Stroll with the TV News"]. Poland, 2006.

Mandela, Nelson. *Long Walk to Freedom.* New York: Little, Brown, 1994.

Marking, Havana (director). *Afghan Star.* UK, 2008.

Marlow, Joyce. *Captain Boycott and the Irish.* London: André Deutsch, 1973.

Mayer, Jane. *The Dark Side: The Inside Story of How the War on Terror Turned into a War on American Ideals.* New York: Doubleday, 2008.

Merrill, Austin. "Best Feet Forward," *Vanity Fair* (July 10, 2007).

Milgram, Stanley. *Obedience to Authority.* New York: HarperCollins, 1974.

Mitchell, Marcia and Thomas. *The Spy Who Tried to Stop a War: Katharine Gun and the Secret Plot to Sanction the Iraq Invasion.* Sausalito, California: PoliPointPress, 2008.

Mercado, Monina Allarey, ed. *An Eyewitness History: People Power, The Philippine Revolution of 1986.* Manila: James. B. Reuter Foundation, 1986.

Newbeck, Phyl. *Virginia Hasn't Always Been for Lovers: Interracial Marriage Bans and the Case of Richard and Mildred Loving.* Carbondale: Southern Illinois University Press, 2004.

Power, Samantha. *A Problem from Hell: America and the Age of Genocide.* New York: Basic Books, 2002.

Quirijns, Klaartje (director). *The Dictator Hunter.* The Netherlands, 2007.

Reticker, Gini (director). *Pray the Devil Back to Hell.* USA, 2008.

Roberts, Adam, and Timothy Garton Ash, eds. *Civil Resistance and Power Politics: The Experience of Nonviolent Action from Gandhi to the Present.* New York: Oxford University Press, 2009.

Robinson, Jo Ann Gibson. *The Montgomery Bus Boycott and the Women Who Started It.* Knoxville: University of Tennessee Press, 1987.

Rusesabagina, Paul. *An Ordinary Man: An Autobiography.* New York: Penguin, 2006.

Sauvage, Pierre. *Weapons of the Spirit.* USA/France, 1989/2007.

Sharp, Gene. *Waging Nonviolent Struggle: 20th Century Practice and 21st Century Potential.* Boston: Extending Horizons, 2005.

———. *From Dictatorship to Democracy: A Conceptual Framework for Liberation.* Boston: Albert Einstein Institution, 2002/2008.

Schrager, Adam. *The Principled Politician: The Ralph Carr Story.* Boulder, Colorado: Fulcrum Publishing, 2008.

Stoltzfus, Nathan. *Resistance of the Heart: Intermarriage and the Rosenstrasse Protest in Nazi Germany.* Piscataway, New Jersey: Rutgers University Press, 2001.

Suzman, Helen. *In No Uncertain Terms: A South African Memoir.* New York: Alfred A. Knopf, 1993.

Thoreau, Henry David. *Civil Disobedience.* New York: Penguin, 1983.

Todorov, Tzvetan. *The Fragility of Goodness: Why Bulgaria's Jews Survived the Holocaust.* Princeton, New Jersey: Princeton University Press, 2001.

Torture in Brazil: A Shocking Report on the Pervasive Use of Torture by Brazilian Military Governments, 1964–1979. New York: Random House, 1986.

Tripp, Aili Mari. *Women and Politics in Uganda.* Madison: University of Wisconsin Press, 2000.

Tschuy, Theo. *Dangerous Diplomacy: The Story of Carl Lutz, Rescuer of 62,000 Hungarian Jews.* Grand Rapids, Michigan: William B. Eerdmans Publishing, 2000.

Tusty, James and Maureen (directors). *The Singing Revolution.* USA, 2008.

U2/Brian Eno, "Miss Sarajevo," published by Blue Mountain Music Ltd|Opal Music, reproduced by kind permission of the publishers.

Vesilind, Priit, and James and Maureen Tusty. *The Singing Revolution.* Tallinn, Estonia: Varrak Publishers, 2008.

Werner, Emmy E. *A Conspiracy of Decency: The Rescue of Danish Jews During World War II.* Boulder, Colorado: Westview Press, 2002.

Weschler, Lawrence. *A Miracle, a Universe: Settling Accounts with Torturers.* Chicago: University of Chicago Press, 1990.

Williams, Jody, Stephen D. Goose, and Mary Wareham. *Banning Landmines: Disarmament, Citizen Diplomacy and Human Security*. Lanham, Maryland: Rowman & Littlefield, 2008.

Younge, Gary. *Stranger in a Strange Land: Encounters in the Disunited States*. New York: The New Press, 2006.

Zmarz-Koczanowicz, Maria (director). *Major, abo rewolucja krasnali* ["Major, or the Gnome Revolution"]. Poland, 1989.

BIBLIOGRAPHY

Index

INDEX

About the Authors

Steve Crawshaw is international advocacy director of Amnesty International. From 2002 to 2010 he worked for Human Rights Watch, first as UK director and then as United Nations advocacy director.

He was a journalist for many years, first with Granada Television in the UK and then joining the *Independent* at launch in 1986. He reported for the *Independent* on the eastern European revolutions, the collapse of the Soviet Union, and the Balkan wars. Other stories included interviewing Burmese opposition leader Aung San Suu Kyi and witnessing the fall of Serb leader Slobodan Milošević.

John Jackson has directed major international campaigns on human rights, economic justice, antipersonnel landmines, HIV/AIDS, and climate change.

He covered international development issues as head of campaigns at Christian Aid and was a founding member and director of the Burma Campaign UK, meeting Aung San Suu Kyi on several occasions to consult on Burma policy.

He has conducted research in a number of conflict areas in Asia, which included working with refugees and survivors of military conflict.

He is currently vice president of social responsibility for MTV Networks International, developing campaigns across its channels worldwide.